Options for Teaching

Joseph Gibaldi, series editor

The Teaching Apprentice Program

in Language and Literature

Edited by

Joseph Gibaldi and James V. Mirollo

New York   The Modern Language Association of America   1981

Library of Congress Cataloging in Publication Data
Main entry under title:

The Teaching apprentice program in language and
   literature.

   (Options for teaching; 4)
   1. Philology—Study and teaching (Internship)—
United States. I. Gibaldi, Joseph, 1942–
II. Mirollo, James V.   III. Modern Language As-
sociation of America.   IV. Series.
P91.5.U5T4   407'.1173   81–1159
ISBN 0–87352–303–2 (pbk.)   AACR2

Published by The Modern Language Association of America
62 Fifth Avenue, New York, New York 10011

CONTENTS

PREFACE

The training of graduate students to teach at the college level has been traditionally neglected in higher education. When virtually all postsecondary school teaching was conducted by full-time professionals after a substantial period of graduate study, this neglect, rightly or wrongly, seemed of little consequence or at least did not arouse serious widespread concern. Over the past two decades, however, as considerably more college teaching has become the responsibility of graduate students, the demand for rigorous college teacher training programs has increasingly grown among not only educators and graduate students but also legislators and trustees as well as undergraduates and their parents. The primary objective of this volume is to present information and ideas about language and literature teaching apprentice programs that have arisen in response to this demand. Our purpose, therefore, is to inform and to stimulate.

The book is divided into two parts. Part I is based on a profession-wide survey we took in preparation for the volume. We present, first, an objective and detailed report on the survey. After a brief statistical overview, we discuss the current state of teaching apprentice activities in language and literature, emphasizing the nature and structure of programs, funding, categories and states of experience, selection of apprentices, duration of apprenticeship, contractual agreements, compensation of apprentices and their role in departmental governance, types of training, responsibilities of apprentices, teaching materials and equipment available, supervision and evaluation, and role and compensation of coordinators. Part I closes with some polemical conclusions and recommendations based on both our research and our considerable experience in the area. Since they are framed within the context of the complete academic picture, our concluding remarks also address a number of indirectly related, but nevertheless extremely important and relevant, professional questions, including that of job prospects for present and future teaching apprentices.

Consistent with the philosophy and format of the MLA's Options for Teaching series, we offer in Part II a number of invited descriptions of representative and innovative teaching apprentice programs covering such varied areas as writing, literature, linguistics, and languages other than English, including Spanish, French, and German as well as Slavic, East European, and Near Eastern languages. The program descriptions have been arranged alphabetically, principally because we see the language and literature profession as a whole. Despite the wide diversity of activities and despite the repetition that must inevitably occur in a collection of this nature, the reader will nonetheless find that each program included, no matter what the discipline, will contain material of interest and use.

In reading the two parts of the volume, the reader may be somewhat confused by the terminology of the editors and the various contributors. It is not uncommon for members of our profession to use such terms as teaching assistant, teaching intern, teaching associate, teaching fellow, assistant instructor, and coteacher to refer to essentially the same role undertaken by a graduate student. In our title and in Part I, we use the term "teaching apprentice" to indicate anyone receiving experience and training to be a college instructor. We choose this term because it connotes the kind of relationship we believe should exist between teaching graduate students and training faculty members. We employ the term "intern" to refer to students teaching in institutions other than those from which they will receive their graduate degrees. We have not imposed our terminology on the contributors to Part II, however, allowing them instead to make use of the terms they normally employ on their campuses, because such terms often have different meanings in different programs and institutions. Yet the context and the description offered in each case will immediately establish the kinds of activities and roles involved.

Because relatively little has been published on the subject of teaching apprentice programs in language and literature, we have of necessity attempted to aim the volume at a large and diverse audience: to the specialist and the nonspecialist, to those experienced in apprentice activities and those just beginning in the area, to the passionately committed and the merely curious. Needless to say, true specialists will find much that is familiar but also, we hope, much that will interest them, although not in every program description and not on every page. In any event, we sincerely hope that this pioneering effort will help generate more research, thought, and publications devoted to both the general and the more specialized aspects of college teacher training in language and literature.

The volume, along with the related MLA Convention Forum "The Teaching Apprentice Program in Language and Literature: Achievements, Failings, Prospects," held in Houston in December 1980, has benefited from the enthusiastic support and invaluable assistance of a great number of professionally concerned individuals. In addition to the thousands of participants in our survey and the twenty-six contributors to the book, we would like to acknowledge our considerable gratitude to Wayne C. Booth, Ward Hellstrom, Frank Hodgins, Cyril Knoblauch, Clara Lee R. Moodie, Alice C. Omaggio, and Albert Sonnenfeld for their efforts to help call attention to both the project and the important subject of college teacher training; to David P. Benseler for his sensitive and meticulous reading of the manuscript; to Ruth apRoberts, Mills F. Edgerton, Jr., Donna L. Gerstenberger, Harriet W. Sheridan, Janet K. Swaffar, Virginia J. Tufte, and Darwin T. Turner of the MLA's Committee on Teaching and Related Professional Activities for encouraging our work and for sponsoring publication of the volume; and to Walter S. Achtert, Richard Brod, Joel Conarroe, and Judy Goulding of the MLA staff for their advice, support, and editorial and administrative assistance.

Finally, we are aware that the training of graduate students of language and literature, crucial in itself, also impinges on such vital professional issues as curriculum, employment, and public support. We are also aware of the illusory and ultimately self-destructive dichotomies that have been created in our profession: English versus foreign languages, undergraduate versus graduate instruction, composition specialist versus literature specialist, teaching versus scholarship. We will deem the volume a true success if it is received as, and judged, a useful source book of ideas and information about teaching apprentice programs and, even more so, if it makes a positive contribution, however small, toward the resolution of some of the pervasive crises that currently afflict the language and literature profession.

J. G.
J. V. M.

PART ONE: THE CURRENT STATE OF TEACHING APPRENTICE ACTIVITIES IN LANGUAGE AND LITERATURE

Joseph Gibaldi and James V. Mirollo

Introduction: A Statistical Overview

To determine where teaching apprentice activities were taking place and how many graduate students were participating in such activities, we began preparation of this volume in the fall of 1979 with a survey of the more than 6,000 postsecondary school language and literature departments and programs in the United States and Canada that are listed in the files of the Modern Language Association. Since we were aware of some intern programs within departments that did not grant graduate or even baccalaureate degrees, we also included in our mailing all four-year and two-year colleges. Our survey produced information about a significant number of diverse teaching apprentice programs and activities. Of the more than 2,300 responses received, about 1,000 departments and programs reported involvement in some sort of apprentice teaching activities.

We received responses from 751 departments and programs that award graduate degrees—284, the M.A. or its equivalent; 467, the Ph.D. or its equivalent. M.A.-granting departments and programs reported a total of 2,087 graduate students participating in teaching apprentice activities. The size of individual apprentice teaching programs in this group ranged from 1 to 60 graduate students. The maximum figure is somewhat misleading, however, for the second largest program had 35 students. The average number of teaching apprentices within reporting M.A.-granting departments was 7.

As might be expected, the bulk of apprentice teachers—about 80% of those reported in our survey—is composed of graduate students teaching within departments and programs that award the Ph.D. The 467 Ph.D.-granting departments that responded reported a total of 10,368 graduate students participating in teaching apprentice activities, the size of programs in this group ranging from 1 to 142. Ten responding departments—mostly English—had 100 or more apprentice teachers in their classrooms; 23 had 75 or more; 58, 50 or more. The average number of teaching apprentices within reporting Ph.D.-granting departments was 22.

Our survey unexpectedly uncovered another development in the area of apprentice teaching. Although we were specifically studying the involvement of graduate students in teaching apprentice activities, some strictly undergraduate language and literature departments, misinterpreting our questionnaire, reported the use of *undergraduates* in teaching activities. Some 135 departments in four-year and two-year colleges responded that they make use of 664 undergraduate students for teaching purposes. Another 26 departments admitted using undergraduates to teach but did not state the number of such students.

If we add the number of these undergraduates teaching language and literature in four-year and two-year colleges to the reported number of graduate school teaching apprentices mentioned above (and throw in, too, the few miscellaneous cases, such as foreign interns teaching in M.A.-granting departments and graduate school interns teaching at two-year colleges), we arrive at a total of well over 13,000 graduate and undergraduate students reported to us as teaching language and literature in colleges and universities in the United States and Canada. (Since the purpose of this part of the volume is to present objectively the results of our survey, we will reserve comment on these developments for our conclusion.)

Our principal aim in conducting the survey, however, was not to collect statistical data but to identify significant trends in the training of graduate students to teach language and literature at the college and university level. Therefore, from the approximately 1,000 departments that claimed to provide some teaching apprentice activities, we selected about 400 whose teacher training efforts seemed particularly well conceived, organized, and developed, and sent them a second, much more detailed questionnaire about their teaching apprentice programs. More than 54% of these departments responded to the second questionnaire. What follows is a summary of the results of this second survey, conducted in the winter of 1979–80, supplemented by information gathered from our initial survey as well as other sources cited below.

Nature and Structure of Programs

The preponderance of teaching apprentice programs are strictly intradepartmental in nature: English and foreign language graduate students are trained for and assigned to teaching duties in undergraduate courses offered by their departments. Our survey, however, also uncovered a number of programs that are extradepartmental in orientation. A few universities have recently established campus-wide teacher training activities, such as the University of Massachusetts' Center for Instructional Resources and Improvement; Indiana University's Associate Instructor Teaching Skills Program; and the Harvard-Danforth Center for Teaching and Learning. Other teaching apprentice programs rely, by choice or necessity, on interdepartmental or interschool arrangements.

By the very nature of their discipline in relation to traditional structuring of language and literature departments, comparative literature graduate students must often seek teaching apprentice experience in other departments. Hence, students in comparative literature departments or programs at such institutions as the University of Illinois at Urbana, University of Iowa, Stanford University, and Carleton University in Ottawa often teach undergraduate courses in English, French, German, Italian, Latin, linguistics, Portuguese, and Spanish that are offered by the individual language departments. When comparative literature departments do have undergraduate course offerings, such as at the University of California at Berkeley, they of course attempt to engage their own graduate students in such courses as much as possible.

On the other hand, small departments and programs that do not award graduate degrees sometimes look to graduate students from other departments to assist in the teaching of their undergraduate courses. The teaching apprentices in the Department of East Asian Languages and Literatures at the University of Oregon, for example, are all graduate students in other departments. Similarly, although the African Studies Center at Michigan State University does not offer degrees, it supports the teaching of African languages by making funds available to hire graduate degree candidates in other programs and departments.

As interest in teacher training has increasingly grown over the past few years, there have been a number of significant efforts at several campuses to combine the resources of related departments to strengthen and enrich teaching apprentice activities. For instance, the foreign language departments at Ohio State University have banded together to offer a two-week preservice orientation course. Likewise, Cornell University's Department of Modern Languages and Linguistics sponsors an interdepartmental summer training program for new and continuing students selected to be apprentice teachers; its participants represent various language departments in the university. The English and Linguistics Departments of the University of Connecticut have agreed to combine their teaching apprentice activities. In its School of Arts and Sciences, New York University's Department of English benefits from assistance from the School of Education and reports that it trains apprentice teachers "with substantial cooperation with English Education."

Activities that encompass two separate campuses constitute another important trend in the area of teacher training. One form of such interschool ventures is the intrauniversity arrangement. A typical example here is the City University of New York, a huge complex of two-year colleges, four-year colleges that grant bachelor's as well as master's degrees, and a graduate center that awards the Ph.D.—all situated within a relatively small geographical area. The CUNY Graduate Center supplies dozens of fellows, adjuncts, and apprentice teachers to language and literature departments throughout the City University system. Sometimes, too, M.A. candidates at the four-year colleges are allowed teaching apprentice experience at one of the two-year colleges. The Claremont Graduate School English Department also attempts to place students in teaching positions at the undergraduate Claremont Colleges. Rutgers University, which now includes a number of colleges throughout the state of New Jersey, seems to be moving in a similar direction.

The most interesting and innovative of these interschool arrangements are those that allow graduate students to teach in a totally different academic environment, including the two-year college, thus permitting them to gain diverse teaching experience that may well enhance their future employment prospects. The English Departments of East Carolina University, Central Michigan University, and the State University of New York at Binghamton are among the relatively few universities that offer programs (complete with internships) specifically for junior and community college teaching. (For a complete listing of such programs in English, see the annual directory issue of *Teaching English in the Two-Year College*, published by East Carolina University.) Graduate students in the English Department at Wright State University may elect a two-year college option that provides an opportunity to teach off-campus for one quarter at a community college, technical college, business college, or university branch campus in the Dayton, Ohio, area. Part of the D.A. program offered by the English Department of the State University of New York at Albany is a required semester-long internship, either full-time or part-time, which also is usually at another institution. Teaching apprentices in the Spanish Department of the University of California at Davis sometimes teach doctors and medical interns in the Individualized Spanish Program at the Sacramento Medical Center. The English Department of Bowling Green State University occasionally makes arrangements for teaching internship positions at nearby colleges or at the two-year Firelands College branch in Huron, Ohio. The M.A. program offered by the Humanities Department of Pennsylvania State University, Capitol Campus, has a built-in junior college internship, generally at Harrisburg Community College, that requires a semester of supervised teaching experience. The English Program of East Texas State University's Department of Literature and Languages sometimes has students who serve as interns in the Dallas Community College system. Finally, graduate students in the Linguistics Department at California State University, Fullerton, teach as interns in community colleges in the area, especially in English as a Second Language (ESL) programs.

Significantly, many two-year schools seem to have taken the initiative in enlisting the assistance of graduate students from nearby schools and, in turn, allowing the students an opportunity to gain valuable teaching experience and often training as well. A pioneer in this area has been the English Department of Kingsborough Community College, which has had since 1968 an intern program that draws from graduate schools throughout the New York City area. Also on the East Coast, Merrimack Valley College has had an agreement with the Graduate Department of Reading at the University of New Hampshire to have graduate students serve its English program by working with freshmen with poor reading skills; Nassau Community College has used English Ph.D. candidates from the State University of New York to tutor students in its remedial writing workshop; the Community College of Baltimore's Department of English, Speech, and Foreign Languages has had teaching interns from neighboring schools such as Loyola College, Johns Hopkins University, Towson State University, and Morgan State University; and J. Sargeant Reynolds Community College has enlisted in its English program some interns from the M.A. program at Virginia Commonwealth University.

In the Midwest, Vincennes University Junior College in Indiana has hired reading interns from some of the major universities in its region. The English Department of Indiana University Northwest has used interns from the University of Chicago's graduate school. Parkland College in Illinois has accommodated in its Communications Division teaching interns from the University of Illinois and the State University of Iowa, while the Humanities Division of

Northern Iowa Area Community College reports that it has made use of interns from the University of Iowa to work in career programs for students in nursing and air conditioning–refrigeration.

Such interschool arrangements are probably most common in California, with its extensive two-year college system. Graduate students from the University of California at Los Angeles have frequently been interns at nearby schools like Los Angeles Pierce College and West Los Angeles College. Grossmont College, Division of Communication Arts, has drawn students from San Diego State University, whereas to the north of the state De Anza College, Language Arts Division, has worked with interns from Stanford University and San Jose University.

Funding

The funding of teaching apprentice programs, like the nature and structure of such activities, is usually a strictly departmental matter. In most cases, part of the department's budget is set aside for the training, supervision, and compensation of apprentice teachers. Occasionally, funds are available from other school or university sources. Brown University's Slavic Department, for instance, has received extradepartmental funding in the form of student support from its graduate school, and the English Department of Bowling Green State University has been the recipient of "regular" and "minority" allocations from the BGSU Graduate College.

In some universities and departments, special funds have been established specifically for teacher training. From 1974 to 1978 the University of California invested over $470,000 in its teaching apprentice training programs. Through the University of California Undergraduate Instructional Improvement Funds, the Spanish Department at the Davis campus, to cite one example, has been able to develop video programs, culture units, a manual, workshops, and other teacher apprentice materials and activities. The TA Workshop of the Department of Slavic Languages and Literatures at the Berkeley campus has also been funded by these instructional improvement grants. At Texas Tech University the English Department has set up its own Basic English Fund, derived from the sale of student guides, which is used in part for teaching apprentice activities.

Although governmental agencies and private foundations would seem likely sources for the improvement of teacher training at the college level, very few apprentice programs seem to have ventured into this area. Our survey has uncovered only a handful of such attempts. In 1968 Kingsborough Community College's English Department applied for and received funds under the Education Profession Development Act (now defunct) to establish its experimental intern program. In the 1979–80 academic year the Department of Literature and Languages at East Texas State University, which offers an Ed.D. in the College Teaching of English, had five teaching apprentices funded by a grant from the National Endowment for the Humanities. Ohio State University has received $875,000 from the NEH to individualize lower division foreign language courses; much of this sum went to the TA Training in Individual Instruction program.

The University of Southern California's English Department has received from the Fund for the Improvement of Postsecondary Education (FIPSE), established in 1972 by the U.S. Department of Health, Education, and Welfare, a grant of $30,000 over two years to help fund the training of teaching apprentices. The Queens English Project, an ambitious collaborative writing program undertaken by Queens College in New York City and a number of high schools within the borough of Queens, is also funded by FIPSE. The project provides apprentice teachers at the college with valuable supplementary training in the teaching of writing.

Foundation support of teaching apprentice activities has been reported at the University of Michigan, Stanford University, the University of Louisville, Cornell University, Yale University, and Drake University. A five-year grant from the Danforth Foundation (St. Louis) allowed the University of Michigan to set up its training program in departments representing the humanities, the social sciences, and the natural sciences. A Danforth grant in excess of a million dollars enabled Stanford to create a Center for Teaching and Learning in 1975. The Summer Institute for Teachers of Composition, sponsored by Louisville's English Department, has received grants from both the university's Toward Greater Quality Fund and the William Bingham Foundation (Cleveland). Likewise, Cornell's six-week Graduate Assistant Training Program in Modern Foreign Languages, held each summer, has been supported in part by grants from the Exxon Education Foundation (New York). With the aid of a grant from the Pew Memorial Trust Foundation in Philadelphia, Yale University has recently strengthened its writing program, including the introduction of a new course for apprentices, The Teaching of Writing. Lastly, as this all too brief survey of reporting departments and programs that have applied for and received extramural funding for teacher training efforts concludes, a grant from the Carnegie Foundation for the Advancement of Teaching (New York) has assisted the English Department at Drake University in its teaching apprentice activities. Although the grant has now expired, the department reports that it has applied for other outside funding.

Categories and Stages in Programs

Many language and literature departments provide graduate students with a wide array of teacher training experiences. East Carolina University's English Department offers not only the traditional teaching apprenticeship experience on its own campus but also internships at two-year colleges. The University of Alabama strives to give each English graduate student training in tutoring in the writing lab as well as in the teaching classroom. The large, complex English program at the University of Iowa is subdivided into a number of programs: Writers Workshop, Literature Core, Rhetoric, American Studies, Afro-American Studies, and Advanced Writing. Each makes use of teaching apprentices, and each provides, too, a variety of teaching experiences and responsibilities. Apprentice teachers in the Rhetoric Program, for example, may tutor in the Reading Lab or the Writing Lab in addition to their regular assignments, whereas those in the Literature Core Program sometimes spend a portion of their apprenticeship grading papers for professors with large lecture classes.

Such assignments are very common for graduate students in language and literature. Like many other English departments, Brigham Young University's regularly assigns apprentices to serve as laboratory instructors and tutors. At Brandeis University, on the other hand, teaching apprentices often assist in grading papers from literature courses taught by regular faculty members. Similarly, two categories of apprentice teachers in the Department of Germanic Studies of the University of British Columbia are Graduate Teaching Assistants and Graduate Staff Assistants. According to the university's statement of policy regarding graduate student service appointments, a chief responsibility of the latter group is marking papers. Both kinds of supplementary assignments are found at the University of Virginia's English Department, which reports, "Many of our TAs get experience as graders for upper division courses or as tutors in our Writing and Reading Center."

Several departments also attempt to include in their teacher training programs experience in diverse classroom situations. A "teaching fellow" in the Harvard English Department may serve as a tutor, a section leader for large lecture courses, and a teacher of a regular course, such as Expository Writing or Introduction to English Literature. In addition to teaching composition courses, graduate students in English at Johns Hopkins University may also teach section discussions for lecture courses. The Slavic Department of Brown University asks its teaching apprentices to lead both oral practice sections in language and discussion sessions in literature. The categories of experience in the apprentice teaching program of the University of Louisville's Department of English include work as "department service assistants" (i.e., principally responsible for developing course materials), tutors in the writing clinic, and instructors of composition, technical writing, and occasionally world literature survey courses.

In some of the more sophisticated programs, it is more proper to speak not of categories but of stages—that is, a series of sequentially arranged pedagogical experiences that forms a common training program for all teaching apprentices. In their most elementary form, such graduated programs require a term or year of closely supervised teaching followed by autonomous teaching with minimal supervision (e.g., Department of Foreign Languages, Arizona State University, and Department of Asian Languages, University of Hawaii at Manoa).

Yet many schools and departments hesitate to place an inexperienced teaching apprentice in front of a classroom, even with close supervision. At Southwest Missouri State University, for instance, graduate students with no previous teaching experience must work with students in a lab situation before they can teach a class. The basis for this system, as noted by the school's chairman of English, is "university policy that no one without prior full-time teaching experience can be unleashed upon students."

Some campuses within the University of California have adopted a similar approach. Four language and literature departments at the Berkeley campus—Comparative Literature, English, Scandinavian, and Slavic—report programs in which "teaching assistants" may be promoted to "teaching associates." New comparative literature teaching apprentices at Berkeley must work along with a "head teacher" and are allowed to teach one literary work during the term. As set down in the basic policies governing the "teaching assistantship" in Berkeley's English apprenticeship program, directed by Charles Muscatine, "Teaching assistants are expected to participate fully with the instructor in charge of their section in all the activities of the course." Specific responsibilities include attending class regularly, preparing along with the class and the instructor, grading about two-thirds of written work, conferring with all members of the class, and teaching the course for at least two full weeks during the term. If successful, the "teaching assistant" may be selected in future terms to be a "teaching associate" (i.e., having autonomous teaching responsibility). The English departments at two other University of California campuses similarly report the following sequences: "an apprenticeship, then a regular classroom assignment" (Riverside) and "an internship with faculty members, then class under loose supervision" (Santa Barbara).

First-year teaching apprentices of English at Marquette University assist professors in large sophomore literature courses: they mark papers, teach two or three classes per term, and hold office hours to confer with students. In the second year of the program the apprentice moves on to supervised autonomous teaching of freshman composition. Likewise, beginning apprentices in the Department of Germanic Languages at the University of Texas at Austin assist a professor for three or four semesters, grading papers, constructing exams, holding office hours, doing tutorial duty, and participating in the department's undergraduate extracurricular activities. After completion of thirty graduate credits, the teaching apprentice may become an independent teacher. The Departments of English at Boston University and Classics at the University of Colorado report parallel sequences, with apprentices in the latter serving first as assistants in mythology or word-study courses, then progressing to autonomous teaching of elementary and intermediate language courses.

Novice apprentice teachers in some programs are frequently required or encouraged, before actual teaching, to participate in activities other than assisting senior faculty members. In English programs such activities usually include serving as a tutor in a learning center (e.g., Columbia University) or a writing workshop (e.g., Drake University). At Colorado State University apprentices work in a remedial lab and a small fundamentals workshop for one semester before assuming "stand-up duties in the required composition class." Besides doing lab work, foreign language teaching apprentices sometimes begin their apprenticeship in "drill" sessions. In the Georgetown University Department of Spanish, to cite but one example, a "drill master" works with a small group of students for two or three hours each week, reviewing and working on material assigned by the teacher of the students' course.

Finally, there are some departments that incorporate these valuable pre-teaching experiences within fully developed teacher training courses. Observation of senior instructors and actual practice teaching are essential components of Cornell's much cited Summer Graduate Assistant Training Program in Modern Foreign Languages. The teacher training course offered by the University of Michigan Department of Near Eastern Studies also involves class observations and practice teaching. All graduate students applying for teaching apprenticeships in the Department of French and Romance Philology at Columbia University must take a course in instructional methods that includes frequent classroom visits and subsequent discussions of the observations. Performance in the methods course is later used as one criterion for selecting students to be apprentices the following year.

Selection of Apprentices and Duration of Apprenticeship

Nearly 75% of graduate departments and programs that responded to our second questionnaire reported the use of students as teaching apprentices during their first year of graduate study. Speaking for many other respondents in our survey, one chairman of a department of foreign languages confessed, "This is more by necessity than choice, since we have been understaffed in recent years and have had to put new TAs into the classroom in their first quarter." Yet some universities, departments, and individuals, struggling to preserve their ideals in a dispiriting world of continual budgetary crises, remain convinced that the practice of employing first-year graduate students to teach is unfair not only to the undergraduate being taught but to the teaching apprentice as well. Percy G. Adams, who directs the English apprentice program at the University of Tennessee, asserts flatly, "We do not let first-year graduate students teach." In this and many other departments, teaching begins in the second year. Among those departments that do not allow their students to become apprentices until their third year of graduate study are the English Department of Harvard, Classics Department of Princeton, English Department of the University of Virginia, and French Department of Yale. Some departments accept only Ph.D. candidates with the M.A. into their apprentice programs. These include the Department of Comparative Literature of the University of California at Berkeley, the Department of Classics of the University of Colorado, and the English Departments of Boston University, University of California at both Berkeley and Riverside, University of Chicago, Columbia University, and University of Wisconsin.

The process of selecting teaching apprentices is just as troubling to some of our respondents as the admission of beginning graduate students into apprentice programs. Comments from a few program directors were particularly candid and revealing. When asked how students were selected to be in the teaching apprentice program, one response was a terse, "Supply and demand." Maintaining the metaphor, another program director admitted, "At present it's a seller's market for graduate students; we almost have to offer an assistantship to anyone we really want to come here." "To be honest, come one, come all," pipes in a third respondent. "Given the dwindling enrollments in our graduate program, almost everyone seeking admission is accepted as a graduate student and awarded a teaching assistantship." Perhaps most poignant and telling of all was the comment received from a foreign language department: "Whoever applies to graduate school gets an assistantship, and many times, unfortunately, we hire people 'off the street.' "

Thus, more often than departments would probably care to acknowledge, entrance to the graduate program also means entrance to the teaching apprentice program. When asked to state the criteria by which graduate students are selected to be in the apprentice program, respondents accordingly listed requirements routinely used for acceptance to graduate study: academic record, teacher recommendations, and Graduate Record Examination scores.

Numerous departments attempt to bring into their selection of apprentice teachers other relevant criteria. Interviews are often arranged, but these prove impractical for graduate applicants in distant geographical locations. Previous teaching experience was cited less frequently than one would expect, but among the many departments that used prior teaching as an important criterion for acceptance into the apprentice program were English, University of Minnesota; Foreign Languages and Literatures, Southern Illinois University; Linguistics, Southern Illinois University; Romance Languages, University of Tennessee; Spanish and Portuguese, Tufts University; German, Washington University; and English, Western Washington University.

Departments that insist on preteaching training often use the experience itself as a method of gauging the teaching promise and commitment of would-be apprentices. Students must first be recommended by their professors for the apprentice program in the Department of French and Italian at Brigham Young University, for example, and subsequently "go through a recruitment workshop where they have a chance to demonstrate both their command of the language and their pedagogical potential." The French and Romance Philology Department of Columbia, the German Department of Harvard, and the Spanish and Portuguese Departments of both Tufts and Yale similarly offer preteaching methods courses that serve to help the departments in selecting graduate students to be teaching apprentices.

Actual testing of students to evaluate basic skills in their field before assignment to classroom duty is fairly infrequent but, for numerous reasons, apparently becoming more and more common. In foreign language departments, competency in the language is often monitored. When considering a student for an apprenticeship, the German Department of the University of Wisconsin insists that "the person's German is good enough." Other departments state that they are likewise concerned with "evidence of ability to speak the language reasonably well" (Modern Languages and Linguistics, Florida State University), "fluency in the language" (French and Italian, Indiana University), "language proficiency" (Germanic Languages, Indiana University), and "competence in the language being taught" (Oriental Studies, University of Pennsylvania).

Modern technology has made it possible to some extent to judge language fluency without an actual interview. The University of Oklahoma's Department of Modern Languages and Literatures uses "tapes made by the applicant in the language in which he or she wants employment." Such tapes are also requested by the Asian Languages and Literatures Department, University of Iowa; Spanish and Italian Department, University of Kentucky; and German Department, Pennsylvania State University. Penn State's Spanish program asks its apprenticeship applicants for a "cassette tape of their Spanish (and English, in the case of foreign students)." The Department of East Asian Languages of the University of Hawaii at Manoa also requires a "tape recording to verify bilingual fluency in English and the target language."

To become an apprentice in the French and Italian Department at the University of Minnesota, a student must not only submit a tape recording but also pass a language screening examination. Formal testing is required in Georgetown's Russian Department and Harvard's Department of Germanic Languages and Literatures. Students in the former must demonstrate competence in oral and written Russian; in the latter department they must pass a language proficiency examination in addition to the successful completion of the preteaching methods course.

In English departments applicants for teaching apprentice programs must often demonstrate their writing ability. Some departments indirectly evaluate an applicant's proficiency in writing. Texas Tech asks applicants to write about their philosophy of education and writing, and reports that the students' writing is "very revealing about their ease and ability in written communication." Bowling Green State requests a written statement of goals, whereas Columbia uses a five-page application requiring discursive responses to questions about teaching composition.

More direct methods of evaluation are employed at Colorado State, the University of Minnesota, and Pennsylvania State, all of which require writing samples as part of the applications. Most direct of all, Brigham Young University actually administers to applicants "some basic tests in grammar and mechanics." Middle Tennessee State likewise has admissions tests; San Francisco State, written and oral exams.

If language and literature departments are generally too eager to accept graduate students into teaching apprentice programs, they seem on the whole rather reluctant to let them go, particularly Ph.D. candidates. Over three-fourths of the M.A.-granting departments that responded to our second survey allow graduate students to serve as apprentice teachers for no more than two years. A few departments let M.A. candidates remain on as apprentices for three or even four years. Three departments of English that award the M.A. only—the University of Puerto Rico, Western Illinois University, and Western Washington University—permit the duration of the apprenticeship to be no more than one year.

On the other hand, nearly 60% of the Ph.D.-granting language and literature departments responding to our follow-up survey stated that they allow graduate students to be apprentices for four or five years. (As much as a fifth of the Ph.D.-granting group permitted apprenticeships of six, seven, or eight years or otherwise acknowledged that the duration was "open-ended"—i.e., until the completion of the dissertation.) The following departments, both large and small in size, reported that their Ph.D. candidates may serve as teaching apprentices for two years or fewer: English, Baylor University; Scandinavian, University of California at Berkeley; English, Columbia University; Linguistics, University of Connecticut; French and Italian, University of Pittsburgh; Classics, Princeton University; Slavic, University of Washington; and French, Yale University.

Contractual Agreements, Compensation, Role in Departmental Governance

In an age and nation of widespread trade unionism, it is perhaps surprising that unions have so little presence or influence in agreements between teaching apprentices and the departments and schools they serve. There is almost always a signed piece of paper, usually with an accompanying statement of the responsibilities of the apprentice, but few departments seem to have developed formal procedures for dealing with real or alleged breaches of contract.

The University of British Columbia is one school that has set down for all its graduate departments a policy for complaint and appeal procedures. Its Statement of Policy regarding Student Service Appointments states that an "aggrieved student" should first attempt to achieve correction of the problem by "consultation with his faculty service supervisor." The next source of redress, according to the policy, is the head of the department. The university urges all departments to have "informal or formal arrangements for identifying and responding to problems that arise within the area of graduate students in a 'service' capacity." These arrangements, the statement continues, "should be such as to ensure speedy consideration of matters brought before it" and may include establishing small committees composed of both faculty members and graduate students. The university policy concludes by stating that appeal beyond the departmental decision "shall be directed to the Dean of the Budget Faculty."

Each teaching apprentice in the Core Literature Program of the University of Iowa is issued a manual setting forth the responsibilities of the apprentice and the department as well as the policies pertaining to the program. Here, too, clear grievance procedures seem to have been worked out. The relevant paragraph reads as follows:

> Graduate Assistant Dismissal Policy states the conditions and the procedures by which a teaching assistant might be removed from his appointment, guaranteeing academic due-process, fairness, and review procedures for all concerned. If conflicts of judgment arise which cannot be otherwise resolved, the Operations Committee provides an additional, objective judgment advisory to the director of the program. A panel of six persons (three faculty, three teaching assistants) randomly chosen from the committee can, if need arises, pass final judgment.

Teaching apprentices on a few campuses have joined together and actually formed unions of their own. At the University of Wisconsin apprentices serve under a contract negotiated between the university and the Teaching Assistants Association, which was formed in 1966. Similarly, the English Department of McMaster University in Hamilton, Ontario, reports, "The graduate students have recently unionized. The union, which is known officially as the Graduate Assistants Association, is now the official bargaining unit under the labour relations act. When the TA indicates acceptance of our terms in a letter, he or she has in fact signed a contract that would stand up in court."

Another new direction in this area is the absorption of the concerns of apprentices by existing college teachers' unions. Apprentice teachers at the University of Oregon, for example, are represented by the American Federation of Teachers. Kingsborough Community College's interns, like all adjunct faculty within the City University system, are covered by the university's contract with the faculty's union, the Professional Staff Congress.

The lack of widespread unionism in teaching apprentice programs has no doubt had its influence on the financial compensation received by apprentices, which one respondent in our survey accurately described in two words: "Not enough!" There are three general types of compensation: (1) full or partial tuition remission alone, which is rare; (2) stipend only, out of which a student must pay full tuition; and (3) a combination of full or partial tuition remission and a stipend. Although few departments divulged the amounts of the stipends they award, those that did reported a range that is very wide indeed. A dozen or so departments that award a stipend alone—all within state universities—revealed amounts that ranged from $3,700 to $6,000 per year for approximately the same work load. Even within single universities we discovered marked differences in amounts of stipends given. At one major Midwest university, for instance, the English Department awards a stipend of $4,800 to its apprentices for teaching three courses per year, whereas their counterparts in the foreign language departments receive $6,000 for a similar course load.

The combination of full or partial tuition remission with a stipend seems the most common form of compensation for teaching apprentices at present. Here, too, practices and amounts differ considerably. Partial remission, for example, may mean 60% at one school, two-thirds at another, or "$7.00 a quarter hour" at a third. The following actual examples, taken from our survey, will give some idea of not only the compensation being offered by some language and literature departments but also the widely varying amounts awarded:

> tuition (up to twelve hours) + $2,800 stipend
> tuition (up to twelve hours) + $4,000 stipend
> full tuition + $1,200 per course
> full tuition + $3,700
> full tuition + $5,200 stipend
> full tuition + $6,200 stipend
> full tuition + $8,400 stipend

Needless to say, the final two or three examples are well above average. The last is a program that has had some outside funding, some of which may well have been channeled into the compensation of apprentices.

Just as teaching apprentices are generally undercompensated for their labors, so they are more often than not underrepresented in overall departmental governance, including curriculum development. The very thought of participation by apprentices in policy-making decisions seemed preposterous to a few respondents. To our question "Do apprentice teachers play a role in departmental governance?," one program director replied, "No, they are not teachers in the department but students." Another added, "Good God, NO!"

Still, it would seem that a growing number of teaching apprentice programs are encouraging apprentices to assume a role, be it formal or informal, direct or indirect, in departmental governance. In some cases, their interests are represented only through the department's graduate student committee or association, which often has a voice and/or vote in some, if not all, departmental matters. Yet often apprentices have representation as apprentices.

In the University of Iowa's English program, teaching apprentices of rhetoric play a formal advisory role. Six of them are elected to an Advisory Board of apprentices and faculty. A similar body has been established as part of the English teaching apprentice program, directed by Paula Johnson and Cyril Knoblauch, at New York University. Six apprentices, "paid extra for their time and effort," serve as an advisory group to "review textbooks, plan curricula, advise about procedures, and help in orienting new teachers."

Some English departments report that they encourage apprentices to play a formal role at departmental meetings. At Brandeis teaching apprentices send "representatives to department meetings who can speak but not vote." At

Baylor "they have a voice and vote in nearly every departmental decision." Mills College permits apprentices to have one representative who is a voting member in department meetings. English teaching apprentices at St. Louis University are all invited to attend meetings and collectively have two votes. In departmental meetings at Rutgers, each apprentice has one-half or one-third vote.

Teacher apprentice participation in decision-making extends, at many schools, to serving on department committees. The German Department of the University of Minnesota allows representation on almost all important committees, particularly encouraging participation in decisions on language programs. Teaching apprentices of German at the University of Arizona and Ohio State University have a representative on every departmental committee except the Faculty Promotion and Tenure Committee. The University of Kentucky's Department of Spanish and Italian reports that its apprentices sit in on all department committees. In the Spanish, Italian, and Portuguese Department of the University of Illinois at Urbana, "they have voice and vote on all departmental committees as well as voice only in faculty meetings."

Numerous English departments follow parallel courses. Apprentices of English at Texas Tech attend faculty meetings and have voting privileges on most important committees. At Kent State University they elect representatives to serve on all departmental committees and vote in most, but not all, matters; at Miami University of Ohio representatives are elected by their peers to all policy-making committees. One apprentice participates in "each major departmental standing committee" at East Texas State University.

Many English departments, like their counterparts in foreign languages, allow apprentices to serve only on those committees that directly pertain to their teaching responsibilities. For example, at the University of Arkansas one elected representative is on each course committee, whereas at Brigham Young apprentices elect a representative to serve (without vote) on the department Composition Council. Duke University permits two teaching apprentices on its Graduate Advisory Committee and two on its Freshman English Committee, where they "assist in choice of textbooks and development of syllabus for Freshman English." The following departments likewise have apprentices serve on graduate committees as well as freshman English (or composition) and textbook committees: University of California at Santa Barbara, Colorado State University, McMaster University, Wright State University, and University of Wyoming.

Prior and Concurrent Training: Courses, Workshops, Orientation Programs

The practice of greeting a newly arrived graduate student with a textbook and a room assignment seems to have (almost) disappeared. Preteaching training, though of varying quality and intensity, is now widely available. As mentioned above, those teaching apprentice programs organized into stages offer experience such as tutoring, grading papers, working with a senior faculty member, practice teaching, and serving as leader of a discussion or drill session before autonomous teaching.

Another option becoming increasingly common is the orientation program before actual teaching. Such activities range from a one- or two-day "crash orientation" through a "one-week professional development seminar" and a "two-week intensive workshop" to the Cornell six-week summer program. Orientation sessions may include theoretical instruction, demonstration lectures, videotapes of master teachers, practice teaching, "micro-teaching" of peers, and distribution of information regarding administrative procedures.

The orientation program at all too few schools is, again as stated above, a full-semester course taken the term before the teaching assignment. We have already mentioned the preteaching methods courses required by the French Department and German Department at, respectively, Columbia and Harvard. Teaching apprentices in the Colorado State English Department tutor in the remedial writing lab as well as take "a three-credit course in how to teach their composition course before they teach it." The Division of Undergraduate Literature at the University of Illinois, directed by Frank Hodgins, reports, "Before assignment to a literature course, a TA successfully completes a professional seminar in the teaching of literature, and this includes the observation of classes taught by faculty members and the opportunity to teach one or two hours himself, in addition to developing a complete syllabus for the course he is to teach the following semester."

In a few departments a nonpedagogical course is a prerequisite to teaching. In the Department of Slavic Languages and Literatures at the University of California at Berkeley the course Descriptive Russian Grammar and a TA Workshop are required prior to appointment. Similarly, Brigham Young University's French and Italian Department has preteaching recruitment workshops and training workshops and requires applicants to "have taken, or be taking, advanced grammar and phonetics." At Marquette, English teaching apprentices who have not had the History of the English Language course must take it before or during their first semester of teaching.

One of the more ambitious series of courses for apprentices is that offered by Harvard's English Department. In the first term of their first year, graduate students must take the course The Teaching and Criticism of Literature, which involves "(a) acquaintance with all the major approaches to literature from classical antiquity to the present; (b) acquaintance with the history of methods and aims of college teaching of literature from the founding of departments in the 1890s to the present; and (3) some practice teaching with criticism by fellow students." During the next year the graduate students take the course The Theory and Practice of the Teaching of Writing, established in 1979–80, "because of the increasing demand in colleges for teachers with direct experience and knowledge of this subject, and with an eye to the teaching of writing to undergraduates in all fields." The emphasis in this second course is on "the use of models, on problems of outline, structure, phrasing, and methods of instruction and of grading papers." Finally, in the third year, which at Harvard is the first year of actual teaching for English apprentices, the graduate student takes The Teaching of English and American Literature course.

Several other English departments now also offer a number of pedagogical courses for the apprentice, either prior to or concurrent with actual teaching. Since 1973 Yale has had the course The Teaching of Literature and recently has added the complementary The Teaching of Writing. At Middle Tennessee

State University separate seminars are required in the teaching of composition and the teaching of literature, and the following courses are recommended: Modern Rhetoric and Prose Style and Problems in Modern English Usage. Wright State University offers The Teaching of Writing, The Teaching of Literature, and Rhetoric. Concurrent courses in the teaching of composition and the teaching of literature are required at Emory and the University of Alabama. East Carolina offers its regular apprentices the course Problems in Teaching Composition and its community college interns Methods of Teaching English in the Two-Year College.

A good many English departments have available for their apprentices courses only in composition and rhetoric. Kansas State has two such courses: one in the history and theory of rhetoric, the other in composition teaching and practice. At the University of Oklahoma there is a course in composition theory and research. Contemporary Rhetorical Theories and Rhetorical Theory and the Teaching of English are offered at, respectively, New York University and the University of Missouri at Columbia. The following is a sampling of other composition courses available throughout the nation:

> Introduction to the Teaching of Composition (Auburn University)
> Composition Instructors' Workshop (Bowling Green State University)
> Teaching Composition (California Polytechnic State University)
> Composition and Composition Pedagogy (Colorado State University)
> Teaching Composition (Drake University)
> Professional Seminar in Writing (University of Illinois, Urbana)
> Composition for Teachers (University of Kentucky, Lexington)
> Teaching College Composition (University of Maine, Orono)
> Content and Methods for Teaching Composition (Oklahoma State University)
> Problems in Teaching Composition (University of South Florida)
> Teaching Writing (St. Louis University)
> Seminar in Teaching Composition (Stanford University)
> Teaching of College Composition (Texas Tech University)

The University of New Mexico English Department seems among the few departments thus far to offer such a potentially valuable course as Teaching Basic Writing.

The Department of English at Boston University is among those departments that treat the teaching of composition and literature within a single course or seminar. The University of Wyoming similarly offers the course The Practical Teaching of Writing and Literature. Brigham Young University requires the seminar Teaching College Composition and Reading and encourages apprentices to take the courses Teaching Composition and Seminar in College and Adult Reading.

A final type of pedagogical course for English teaching apprentices is that devoted to the general subject The Teaching of College English. Among those departments of English that provide such courses are those of East Texas State University, Kent State University, Lehigh University, North Illinois University, and Virginia Polytechnic Institute and State University.

Needless to say, foreign language departments also require or recommend pedagogical courses to their teaching apprentices. A sampling of course titles:

> Problems of Teaching German (University of Arizona, German)
> German Teaching Methods (Brigham Young University, Germanic Languages)

Teaching Methodology (University of California-Berkeley, Slavic Languages and Literatures)

Problems in Teaching Foreign Languages (Emory University, Modern Languages and Classics)

Foreign Language Education (Florida State University, Modern Languages and Linguistics)

Teaching Methodology (Georgetown University, Russian)

Methods of Teaching College Spanish (Indiana University, Spanish and Portuguese)

Analysis and Teaching of German (University of Minnesota, German)

Teaching College Spanish (University of Virginia, Spanish, Italian, and Portuguese)

Finally, we cite the important training seminars sponsored by the Harvard-Danforth Center for Teaching and Learning. Among its many programs, the Center offers a series of lectures and discussions directed at all Harvard Teaching Fellows. Because its scope is campus-wide, the Center can bring together members of different schools within the university to discuss common problems and to share successful pedagogical methods and approaches. A series of seven weekly seminars, for example, was given by a business school professor on the subject: Developing Discussion-Leading Skills. Other lecture and discussion topics have included Using the Socratic Method in Arts and Sciences and Why Commit Yourself to Teaching When the Payoff Is for Research?

Responsibilities of Apprentices

The principal responsibility of teaching apprentices, by and large, is autonomous classroom teaching, albeit often within strictly prescribed and uniform procedures and course syllabi. Nonetheless, there are some departments that do not assign apprentices complete responsibility for classes, thereby avoiding the disturbing, though omnipresent situation of doctoral candidates replacing as classroom teachers numerous more qualified yet jobless recent Ph.D.s in language and literature. The University of Chicago's English Department, to cite one notable example, permits graduate students to work closely with a senior faculty member, observing classes, participating in the planning of the course, and assuming the teaching of some three to six sessions during the term. Graduate students here serve as true "assistants," never displacing a more qualified and experienced scholar-teacher, and, in fact, receive course credit for the experience. Similarly, the Department of Asian Languages and Literature of the University of Iowa reports that its apprentice teachers "primarily assist a senior professor," and the University of Wyoming's English Department, which assigns each teaching apprentice to a faculty mentor, lists its apprentices' responsibilities as follows: "attend colloquia, attend faculty mentor's composition class, read and report on the literature of composition, grade papers, submit papers for grade monitoring, and work in Writing Center."

Canadian institutions seem to have a well-established tradition of true "teaching assistants." At Queen's University, Ontario, apprentices are tutors assigned to work with course instructors. Their duties are to hold interviews with the undergraduate students in each instructor's class and to grade papers for that instructor. In addition, the tutor may do some practice teaching. The relevant paragraph in the departmental guidelines reads:

> The Department wishes to encourage its graduate students to do some apprenticeship teaching under the experienced eye of an instructor. Although this is completely up to each professor, most of them will invite the tutor to teach from three to five periods in each term on some author or work or unit of interest to the tutor. Normally the instructor will attend some of the tutor's lectures and offer afterward some constructive criticism of his performance. Sometimes, also, the instructor will consult with the tutor about suitable essay topics in these or other areas; this is a practice that is to be encouraged.

The Departments of English at both the University of Calgary in Alberta and Dalhousie University in Nova Scotia also report that the primary responsibility of their apprentices is to assist—not replace—faculty members.

Another step short of completely autonomous teaching by apprentices is assignment to teach supplementary or auxiliary workshops or discussion groups. In Brigham Young's French and Italian Department, which offers only the M.A., apprentices are called "live lab instructors" and are asked to conduct a half-hour laboratory following each "master class"; their role is "to help the students practice and apply what has just been presented in the master class." We have already mentioned that the chief role of apprentices in the Brown University Slavic Department is to lead oral practice sessions in language and discussion sessions in literature.

Besides autonomous teaching, assisting a senior faculty member, tutoring, and grading, teaching apprentices sometimes assume nonteaching duties. These include engaging in departmental service such as course development or editorial work (e.g., each year two English apprentices at Purdue assist in the editorial office of the department's journal, *Modern Fiction Studies*). Occasionally, particularly skilled senior teaching apprentices are asked to help in the supervision of new apprentices.

Not unexpectedly, the kinds of courses to which apprentices are most often assigned are those that are most basic—that is, freshman composition and elementary foreign language courses. Common, too, is assignment to such courses as remedial writing and reading, English as a Second Language, and English for foreign students. At some schools, English apprentices are also asked to teach advanced writing as well as business or technical writing courses; foreign language apprentices teach conversation, translation, and culture courses. Although many graduate students, especially in English, specialize in literature study, they are infrequently assigned to teach literature. Even less common are assignments to courses like film, mass media, myth, and folklore.

The forms and sizes of classes that apprentices teach are generally no different from what established faculty members are accustomed to: lecture classes, recitation sessions, workshops, and so on. The average class size seems to be about twenty-five students, ranging from below ten to as many as forty-five students per class. (One department reported that it assigns a teaching apprentice to a large lecture session of some 200 students.)

Teaching apprentices are usually expected to devote from five to twenty hours a week to the apprenticeship experience. One department has established that apprentices should devote about ten hours per week for each section being taught. Although some departments do not "legislate" apportionment of nonteaching duties, many now do. The following is a sampling of the sorts of schedules prescribed for apprentices at various schools:

> 5 hours teaching + 2 hours conferences + 2 hours language laboratory = 9 hours total
> 5 hours teaching + 5 hours conferences = 10 hours total
> 5 hours teaching + 5 hours conferences + 2 hours observing senior faculty = 12 hours total
> 6 hours teaching + 6 hours conferences and tutoring + 8 hours preparation = 20 hours total
> 4 hours teaching + 16 hours conferences, preparation, grading = 20 hours total

Teaching Materials and Equipment

In addition to providing improved teacher training, many language and literature departments have in recent years made available to their apprentices an impressive array of useful pedagogical materials, including not only textbooks but instructor's manuals, course syllabi, sample lesson plans, handouts, worksheets, and even taped lectures and videotapes of master teachers. For example, the University of New Mexico's Department of Modern and Classical Languages has for its first-year Spanish courses a lesson plan for *each* class of the semester.

Actual "handbooks" for teaching apprentices are now quite common throughout the nation. Schools within the University of California system seem to have been among the pioneers in publishing such handbooks. Available titles include *Tips for TAs* (San Diego), *What Every TA Should Know* (Los Angeles), and *Introductory Notes to TAs* (Davis). In 1977 Stanford University published its *Handbook for Teaching Assistants at Stanford*, edited by Patricia O'Connell Killen and Carrie Walker. This seventy-page bound pamphlet contains a chapter on the "rules and regulations governing student assistantships" at the university, a "TA Information Directory," a list of university publications and courses of value to apprentices, a short bibliography on college teaching, a map of the campus, and a current academic calendar. The chapter entitled "Tips for TAs" offers facts and suggestions concerning such matters as book orders, library procedures, planning and delivering a lecture, leading a discussion section, grading papers, dealing with classroom problems, and preparing for future job seeking.

It should be noted that the magazine *Change*, drawing from the Stanford and UCLA handbooks, published in 1978 the pamphlet *How to Succeed as a New Teacher: A Handbook for Teaching Assistants*. The publication's bibliography and its chapters "Administrative Details," "Teaching," "Evaluation," and "Faculty, Students, Anxiety" were all taken from the *Handbook for Teaching Assistants at Stanford*; scattered throughout these chapters are a few insertions from UCLA's *What Every TA Should Know*. Original material in the *Change* pamphlet includes David Halliburton's essay "A New Deal for New Teachers," a brief overview of the state of teaching apprentice programs, and the section "TA Training Programs," which contains concise descriptions of apprentice activities at eight universities—Michigan, Indiana, Northwestern, California, Wisconsin, Massachusetts, Harvard, and Stanford.

In 1973 Raji M. Rammuny prepared, for the University of Michigan's Department of Near Eastern Languages and Literatures, a *Handbook for Graduate Teaching Assistants and Instructional Assistants*, a bound pamphlet of some seventy-five pages. The Rammuny handbook is divided into two parts: "Policies and Regulations" (e.g., terms and procedures of employment, remuneration, responsibilities, grievance procedures, termination of appointment) and "Methodologies." The second part contains course outlines, lesson plans, sample tests, copies of teacher evaluation forms, pedagogical advice, and a reading list on language teaching and learning. The English Departments of the University of Iowa and Oklahoma State University are among those that have prepared similar manuals for their apprentices, using a less expensive rexograph format. As of this writing, there are indications that some commercial publishers are considering publication of such handbooks and manuals for apprentice teachers.

Several departments also report having established departmental libraries of teaching materials. Often available to apprentices are such pedagogically useful books as:

Allen, Edward D., and Rebecca M. Valette. *Classroom Techniques: Foreign Languages and English as a Second Language.* New York: Harcourt, 1977.

Chastain, Kenneth. *Developing Second-Language Skills: Theory to Practice.* 2nd ed. Chicago: Rand McNally, 1976.

Christensen, Francis, and Bonniejean Christensen. *Notes toward a New Rhetoric.* 2nd ed. New York: Harper and Row, 1978.

Corbett, Edward P. *Classical Rhetoric for the Modern Student.* 2nd ed. New York: Oxford Univ. Press, 1971.

Galyean, Beverly. *Language from Within.* Santa Barbara, Calif.: Confluent Education Development and Research Center, 1976.

Gibson, Walker. *Tough, Sweet, and Stuffy: An Essay on Modern American Prose Styles.* Bloomington: Indiana Univ. Press, 1966.

Grittner, Frank. *Teaching Foreign Languages.* 2nd ed. New York: Harper and Row, 1977.

Hirsch, E. D., Jr. *The Philosophy of Composition.* Chicago: Univ. of Chicago Press, 1977.

Irmscher, William. *Teaching Expository Writing.* New York: Holt, 1979.

Kinneavy, James. *A Theory of Discourse.* Englewood Cliffs, N.J.: Prentice-Hall, 1971.

Moffett, James. *Teaching the Universe of Discourse.* Boston: Houghton Mifflin, 1968.

Ohmann, Richard, ed. *Teaching English in Two-Year Colleges.* Urbana, Ill.: NCTE, 1974.

———, and W. B. Coley, eds. *Ideas for English 101: Teaching Writing in College.* Urbana, Ill.: NCTE, 1975.

Politzer, Robert L., and Frieda N. Politzer. *Teaching English as a Second Language.* New York: Wiley, 1972.

Rivers, Wilga M. *A Practical Guide to Teaching French.* New York: Oxford Univ. Press, 1975.

———, Kathleen Mitchell Dell'Orto, and Vincent Dell'Orto. *A Practical Guide to Teaching German.* New York: Oxford Univ. Press, 1975.

———, Milton M. Azevedo, William H. Heflin, Jr., and Ruth Hyman-Opler.

A Practical Guide to Teaching Spanish. New York: Oxford Univ. Press, 1976.

Seelye, H. Ned. *Teaching Culture: Strategies for Foreign Language Educators.* Skokie, Ill.: National Textbook, 1976.

Shaughnessy, Mina. *Errors and Expectations: A Guide for the Teacher of Basic Writing.* New York: Oxford Univ. Press, 1977.

Tate, Gary, ed. *Teaching Composition: Ten Bibliographical Essays.* Fort Worth: Texas Christian Univ. Press, 1976.

Valette, Rebecca M. *Modern Language Testing.* 2nd ed. New York: Harcourt, 1977.

Young, Richard E., Alton Becker, and Kenneth Pike. *Rhetoric: Discovery and Change.* New York: Harcourt, 1970.

The English Department of the University of California at Berkeley has a Composition Library that contains "composition texts, essay collections, anthologies of literature, a women's literature shelf, editions of Shakespeare's plays, journals, instructor's manuals, and a small number of theoretical works about composition" as well as copies of *Books in Print* and a file of "instructors' favorite assignments and exercises." The departments of English at Colorado State, Cornell, and Wright State also have libraries of composition materials.

Among foreign language departments, the University of Minnesota French and Italian Department provides apprentices with "course syllabi, worksheets, videotapes, sample lesson plans, and pedagogical materials (e.g., journals, articles, books)"; Bowling Green State's Department of German and Russian includes among its "supportive materials" the following: lesson plans, recorded plays, pronunciation exercises, poetry readings, and musical recordings. The Resource Information Center set up by the Comparative Literature Department of the University of California at Berkeley contains dictionaries, textbooks, handbooks on writing, files of teaching materials, art slides, slide projectors, phonographs, and recordings of music and plays.

As is evident, a good many departments provide apprentices with mechanical aids to teaching and often offer formal training in such aids, which include, on the one hand, duplicating machines and other office equipment and, on the other, the full spectrum of audiovisual materials and equipment. Now readily available to many apprentices are posters, visual cards, phonographs, tape recorders, overhead projectors, slide and film projectors, and videotape machines, among other items.

The Brigham Young English Department offers its apprentices a wide variety of pedagogical aids. Its department library includes course syllabi, samples of rhetorical modes, exercises, the Christensen *Rhetoric* on transparencies, cassette tapes, books on teaching composition and reading, publications of the National Council of Teachers of English, and journals such as *College Composition and Communication* and *College English.* At the university's Learning Resources Center, run by the English Department, students have access to many diagnostic and follow-up tests and can also use, at relatively low cost, a completely computerized composition and reading program geared to individual needs.

The Spanish Department of the University of California at Davis makes the following report: "Videotape presentations of difficult structures (*Ser* vs.

Estar, Preterite vs. Imperfect, Direct vs. Indirect Objects, and so on) are available to TAs and students. Also, a large selection of language cards, visual grammar, slide/sound culture units have been developed by TAs over the years in the methods course and are incorporated into the program." Ohio State University's Department of German offers its apprentices "an extensive language laboratory program, the *Guten Tag* film series, filmstrips, slides and a computer-assisted instruction program."

Supervision and Evaluation

Most teaching apprentices in language and literature can rely on their departments for assistance and support in the form of not only material and equipment but also close supervision and frequent consultation. Formal methods courses and opportunities to observe senior faculty, as mentioned above, are widespread; so are more informal workshops and regular (usually weekly) meetings between apprentices and supervisors. English apprentice teachers at the University of Maine at Orono and Virginia Polytechnic Institute and State University are required to keep logs and journals, which are discussed at weekly meetings.

A few departments encourage team work among apprentices, either pairing them off or forming small groups to plan lessons or make up tests. Other forms of the "buddy system" include assigning new teaching apprentices to work with experienced apprentices (e.g., University of Minnesota, German). The German Department of Ohio State has "course captains," advanced apprentices who observe and otherwise assist novices.

Parallel arrangements exist in English departments. One category of apprenticeship in Kent State's Department of English is the "Advisory Teaching Fellow, a teaching assistant of some quality and experience who helps new TAs become acquainted with Kent's program and receives a reduced load for this service." Similarly, at the University of Illinois six apprentices are selected each year to be "rhetoric advisers."

Even more interesting, the Departments of English at Miami University of Ohio, Drake University, Louisiana State University, Texas Tech University, Tulane University, and the University of Alberta, among others, all enlist regular faculty members to serve as "buddies." The Faculty Mentor Program at Miami University is designed "(1) to provide the mentee direct access to an experienced teacher with whom the mentee can discuss the problems and process of teaching; and (2) to fulfill the department's responsibility to supervise student-teachers." Mentors observe mentees at least three times each term, following each observation with a discussion of the session and a written evaluation of the mentee's performance. In the second and subsequent semesters the apprentice is assigned a different mentor. This rotation of assignments is "to allow the broadest possible exposure to teaching styles and philosophies." English apprentices at Drake, Louisiana State, and Texas Tech also work with faculty "mentors." In other departments, faculty members in similar roles are alternately given such titles as "faculty preceptors" (Tulane) and "teaching supervisors" (Alberta).

Other forms of supervision abound. English apprentices at Northern

Illinois must have their syllabi and unit plans approved. The University of Akron's Department of Modern Languages evaluates tests and other materials prepared by apprentice teachers for classroom use. Standards of grading are, of course, of major concern. Consequently, there are paper-grading sessions and cross-grading exercises arranged by the English Departments of, respectively, Boston University and the University of Virginia. The Department of Spanish and Portuguese at the University of Toronto and the University of Wyoming's English Department both report monitoring of grading by apprentices; at California State University at Chico, the University of Iowa, Pennsylvania State University, and elsewhere, sets of graded compositions are regularly reviewed.

An important aspect of the supervisor's work is the professional evaluation of an apprentice teacher's performance, essential not just for the purposes of reappointment and future recommendations but for the enlightenment and professional growth of the apprentice as well. Student evaluations, though commonly used, are rarely the sole means of evaluating an apprentice's performance. A few departments, like the Department of Germanic Languages at the University of Texas at Austin, permit apprentices to videotape their own classes, attempting thereby to facilitate the objective sought by all teachers: rigorous self-appraisal.

Doubtless the most common form of evaluation is the classroom visitation. Such visits may be solely at the request of the apprentice or, as seems increasingly the norm, may be a mandatory part of the program. Mandatory visitations may be announced or unannounced, and observers may be other apprentices or, as is more usual, regular faculty members. (In the University of Minnesota's English Department, each apprentice is visited by a tenured faculty member as well as a "senior peer.") The number of observers and the number of observations within a given term also vary considerably. Whereas one visitation per term seems the average minimum, apprentices in the Department of Modern Languages at the University of Akron are observed as many as three or four times each semester. The French and Italian Department of the University of California at Berkeley requires four class visits per quarter, the observers including the program supervisor and two other members of the department. At Drake the apprentice is observed twice each term by the Director of Freshman English and once by a faculty mentor.

Technology has altered the form and nature of visitations in many schools. Teaching apprentices in Indiana University's Department of Spanish and Portuguese may be asked to teach in an observation room with a one-way mirror or to videotape or audiotape themselves and prepare an "interaction analysis." Videotaping of apprentices is regularly used in several foreign language departments, such as the University of California at Davis, Spanish; University of Cincinnati, Germanic Languages and Literatures; and University of Minnesota, French and Italian.

Pre- and postobservation analyses and conferences, as well as written evaluations, are usual procedures associated with classroom visitation. Many observers find it useful to have a standard evaluation sheet or a shortened evaluation checklist with which to work. (If shared with teaching apprentices, such forms may also serve to enhance self-evaluation or, at least, help prepare the apprentice for the observation and the ensuing conference.) Categories on the evaluation sheet used by Emory University's Department of Modern Languages and Classics include lesson planning (variety of activities/techniques, objectives given for each activity, mixture of new and familiar material, transitions between activities), techniques used (amount of teacher talk vs. student talk, target language used, errors corrected, use of visuals), class atmosphere (amount of student volunteering, students prepared, interaction between students), analysis (did learning occur? were goals attained?), and strategy (how can successful approach be applied again? how can less successful approach be improved?). The evaluation form used by the Department of Near Eastern Languages and Literatures at the University of Michigan includes preparation and organization of material, teaching techniques used, apprentice's command of target language, use of target language in class, rapport with class, student participation, interaction between teacher and students, pace, and class atmosphere.

Written evaluation reports filed with departments now often become part of the graduate student's permanent dossier. An interesting practice recently adopted by Harvard's Department of English and American Literature and Language should be noted in concluding this section. The dossier of each Ph.D. from that department includes a form letter signed by the current department chairman, David Perkins, and the Director of Placement, Jerome H. Buckley. The letter begins with the following statement: "Harvard views the knowledge and experience of teaching to be an integral part of the preparation for the Ph.D., as a necessary supplement to scholarly expertise." It goes on to describe the three pedagogical courses required of each Ph.D. candidate and the kinds of teaching duties assigned to "teaching fellows" in the department. Attached to the letter is the "record of the candidate's teaching experience and comments on his or her teaching abilities."

Program Coordinators

Our survey found convincing evidence of a major trend in the supervision of teaching apprentice programs in language and literature. (Renate Schulz revealed a similar trend in her recently published report on teacher training in foreign languages, *ADFL Bulletin*, 12, No. 1 [Sept. 1980], 1–8.) As pointed out in M. P. Hagiwara's *Leadership in Foreign Language Education: Trends in the Training and Supervision of Graduate Assistants* (New York: MLA, 1970) and other earlier studies, persons in charge of teaching apprentice operations have usually been the least established members of the staff—generally untenured, sometimes even without the Ph.D. In recent years, however, there appears to have been in the profession as a whole a significant change in the thinking behind the assignment of teaching apprentice coordinators. Close to two-thirds of the departments participating in our second survey reported that fully tenured faculty members were in charge of supervising apprentices— many of them distinguished and widely known members of the profession. One English department boasted that its coordinator of teaching apprentices was "one of the four highest paid members of a department of nearly one hundred."

Although this new development certainly reflects a growing awareness of the importance of teacher training, it has been noted by several that the increasing participation of senior faculty members in apprentice programs may to some extent be due to the "over-tenured" or "tenured-in" state of many language and literature departments, an unfortunate phenomenon that has afflicted the profession in recent years. Then, too, there are still many departments that do not readily assign senior faculty members to supervise apprentices or that do not eagerly grant tenure to those junior faculty members who accept the assignment. In response to the question "Is the supervisor of the program a tenured member of the department?," one program coordinator confided, "Only this year (after a great struggle)—never before." Another department admitted that its apprentice program was "generally run by the three *youngest* teachers."

Compensation of teaching apprentice supervisors seems, accordingly, to be more generous than in the past. Nearly all reporting departments offered one of the following types of compensation: (1) reduced teaching load, (2) additional stipend, and (3) both reduced teaching load and additional stipend. Schedule reduction seems to depend, for the most part, on the size of the program and the extent of the supervisor's role. Smaller departments often offer schedules reduced by one or two courses per term; in larger departments supervisors may have a half-time schedule or even three-quarters reduced time. Reported stipends for apprentice program supervisors ranged from $1,500 to $6,000 a year, although some stipends were tied to such formulas as "one-ninth salary supplement," "half-course equivalent salary," and "every other summer off with pay."

Combinations of stipend and reduced teaching load also vary greatly. A very large department with over one hundred teaching apprentices offers a reduction in teaching load by three or four courses a year, a 5% salary supplement, and an administrative supplement for the summer; in another department with slightly fewer apprentices, the supervisor receives "release from 50% teaching load and added summer stipend." Compensation for one Director of Freshman English who supervises some twenty-six apprentices is "released time of one-third of course load plus $2,000"; for another, who directs a program that includes fourteen apprentices, it is "a stipend of $1,000 and three hours of released time."

Our survey also indicated a trend away from the direction of teaching apprentice programs by a single supervisor. Of course, there are still many departments that assign only one person to direct an entire program, and not infrequently a sizable one. It is clear, nonetheless, that more and more departments are calling on a number of persons to assist in the supervision of apprentice programs. In foreign language departments responsible for the teaching of several languages, it is common for each language area to have its own coordinator of apprentices, but other administrative arrangements also exist. In the Department of Germanic Studies at the University of British Columbia, two faculty members coordinate the apprentice program: a supervisor of language courses, who works on scheduling, and a supervisor of assistants, who is responsible for teacher training. At the University of Georgia, the faculty supervisor of apprentices in the Department of Romance Languages is assisted by a "graduate student preceptor." The larger program in the University of Illinois Department of Spanish, Italian, and Portuguese is supervised by the Language Coordinator and two advanced apprentices who serve as "assistant supervisors." The Department of Modern Languages and Linguistics at

Florida State University has a single supervisor, but "help is solicited from other regular faculty members for class observations." The Lower Division Coordinator administers the training program in the Department of Germanic Languages of the University of Texas at Austin, but other faculty members serve as "course coordinators," working closely to carry on the program in the third and fourth semesters of the apprenticeship.

Many English departments have adopted similar strategies for the administration of apprentice programs. As in many other schools, Wright State's English training program is jointly coordinated by the Director of Freshman English and the Director of Graduate Studies. The English programs at both Purdue and Wyoming have single supervisors assisted by a number of faculty mentors. At the University of Illinois, Urbana, the Director of Freshman Rhetoric and the Director of Undergraduate Literature are joined in their supervisory efforts by other faculty members who serve as "course chairmen." The Colorado State English program has a regular staff of four supervisors: a director of composition, an assistant director in charge of placement, an assistant director in charge of personnel, and a remedial supervisor. East Texas State and Brigham Young also enlist the assistance of four faculty members to supervise English apprentices: Department Head, Coordinator of Freshman Composition, Director of Interns, and Director of Communication Skills at East Texas State; and at Brigham Young, Coordinator and Assistant Coordinator of Composition as well as Supervisors of Writing Laboratory and Reading Laboratory. At the University of Iowa, apprentices are variously supervised by the Director of the Writers Workshop, Director of Literature Core, Coordinator of Rhetoric Program, and Chairmen of the following programs: American Studies, Afro-American Studies, and Advanced Writing.

Finally, Cornell's Emphasis on Writing Program is noteworthy because of its interdepartmental nature. The program has two directors as well as two or three senior staff members who lead seminars for apprentices. Codirector of the program, Robert T. Farrell, Professor of English, Medieval Studies, and Archaeology, described the Cornell project thus:

> Our program is built on the notion that unless a significant number of staff in *all* Humanities programs are involved in teaching writing, we are not doing our students justice. . . . There is a strong cadre of senior people who are very dedicated to the teaching of writing, and we are very pleased that at least half of them are outside the English department.

Polemical Conclusions and Recommendations

It should now be apparent to the reader that a great deal of apprentice activity is going on in many colleges and universities throughout the United States and Canada. A crucial change in attitude is taking place toward the importance of teaching in the preparation of graduate students for the profession. Indeed, considering how research and scholarly specialization have long been the central interest, if not the exclusive preoccupation, of graduate language and literature departments, this change is genuinely significant. But our purpose in this polemical conclusion is to take a searchingly critical look, within the larger academic context, at apprentice activities we have described above, and to offer personal recommendations for addressing some of the problems we believe seriously afflict teacher preparation.

Foremost in our minds is an overwhelming paradox. At the very time when so much attention is being given to teacher preparation there is a continuous shrinkage of employment possibilities in language and literature teaching. In short, we are training our graduate students to develop professional skills that many of them may never have the opportunity to apply after receiving their doctoral degrees. Having pondered this dilemma at some length, we conclude that despite the current depressed state of the academic job market, teacher preparation ought to be further improved and strengthened. After all, no one has argued that there will be *no* jobs in the future; and as long as some teaching positions are available in language and literature departments now and in the near future, they should be filled with the very best trained people. At the same time the number of graduate trainees, no matter how well trained, is a matter of deep concern. Hence we address ourselves first to questions of quality *and* quantity.

Not all current teaching apprentice programs are worthwhile. The programs we have surveyed vary drastically in quality, but those we especially deplore are weak in preparation of their trainees, whom they give little support, perfunctory supervision, and no pedagogical training; under the guise of a preferred informality or a desire to avoid dry pedagogy, they simply put young graduate students in front of a classroom to manage as best they can. Obviously in many institutions teaching apprentices are regarded as little more than cheap labor, although their need for tuition exemption and a stipend in order to pursue graduate studies unfortunately makes them willing victims of this attitude of neglect.

There is also a recognition problem. Even when a program or activity is excellent, we note that in many departments the preparation of teachers tends to be an isolated enterprise. The separation from literary study, the limited involvement of senior faculty, the absence of reward, not to mention tenure prospects, for many engaged in teacher preparation all contribute to giving teacher training an inferior status in such departments—this despite, in a few instances, a fulsome rhetoric that asserts the contrary. One special irony is that some departments' public rhetoric denies the plaintive expressions of neglect we encountered in our survey responses. Because graduate departments are anxious to place their doctoral students and are keenly aware of the new emphasis on teaching, they tend to assert their enthusiasm for teacher preparation in strong and solemn tones. Yet a closer look reveals that the teaching apprentice program they boast of is often an isolated or peripheral area of interest, left almost entirely in the hands of junior faculty and a few veterans who have expressed a "special" or "unusual" interest in this area. It is almost certain, too, that in such circumstances there will be little value placed on research and publication in pedagogical matters.

For example, one professor of Romance languages in the Far West confided, "Teaching preparation, as in so many foreign language graduate programs in these United States, is given rather short shrift in this department. Our preservice and in-service work is perfunctory at best. The senior people are 'into' literature and/or linguistics, so that they (and consequently the graduate students) are indifferent, if not actually opposed, to that 'Education thing.'" A director of writing in the Northeast added, "I would like to make our weekly workshop into a course, and I would like to expand our training program to include more involvement by senior members of the English Department. So far they have been unwilling to do either of these things. The teaching of writing still suffers from the prejudices of professors of literature." Another English professor declared, "Most of our staff simply will not teach composition." Finally, a participant in our study made this suggestion to us: "Your next project ought to try to get at the professors' attitudes toward language instruction, TA training, and supervision of TAs. I expect that, if truth were told, you would find that this highest enrollment portion of the curriculum is neglected or scorned by most tenured faculty."

Another problem we view with alarm is the increasing resort to peer teaching (as opposed to limited peer tutoring). While the use of undergraduates to teach their peers in the classroom is sometimes justified by departments on the grounds of valuable experience and career exploration, we take a dim view of such justifications and indeed of the whole practice of autonomous peer teaching. We suspect that peer teaching is usually motivated primarily by budget considerations and, as such, is exploitation pure and simple. And double exploitation at that, since the students as well as the peer teacher suffer the consequences. In this respect it seems to us merely a lower-level version of the similar problem of having beginning graduate students teach autonomously and automatically as part of their graduate fellowships. Indeed, first-year graduate students who begin teaching immediately on arrival, with little or no preparation, are themselves scarcely more than peer teachers, despite their graduate status. As indicated above, some of the respondents, especially in foreign language departments, were frank enough to admit to us that they felt they had no choice in the matter—in order to have any graduate students at all one has to offer them teaching assistantships or fellowships involving teaching. Or, put another way, in order to staff basic courses cheaply, it is necessary to have a significant number of graduate students on hand.

The reader must have been impressed if not shocked by the statistics in our introduction indicating the large numbers of graduate students currently serving as teaching apprentices all over the country, but especially in large English departments. Since most of these trainees are doctoral candidates heading for the bleak job market, we find ourselves overwhelmed and distressed by the prospect of having so many trained individuals unable to use their training professionally.

It is surely a bitter irony that the employment of large numbers of teaching apprentices has resulted in punishing those apprentices who succeed in completing their graduate work. For, by taking up at a relatively cheap cost the instructional burden of the basic courses, teaching apprentices actually help create the job shortage that will eventually force many of them out of the profession. Indeed, if all the basic courses now taught by teaching apprentices were converted into full-time positions, there would be no job shortage at all! Moreover, since basic courses in language and literature have been virtually handed over by the senior professoriat in many departments to graduate students and part-time and visiting faculty, these courses are, as it were, outside the tenure territory, doomed to be taught perpetually by teaching apprentices and non-tenure-track faculty. In the past, when every basic course in a department's curricular offering was taught by the entire staff, including senior professors, more tenure-track appointments and more tenure slots were available. The existence of a "fluid bottom," especially in large departments, is in good measure due to the newly inferior status of a whole mass of undergraduate basic courses, taught by transients.

Awareness of this kind of exploitation has led some teaching apprentices to organize themselves at several institutions. The resulting collective bargaining contracts have undoubtedly ameliorated working conditions, but they cannot meet the fundamental need to budget permanent teaching positions, and indeed they may have the effect of guaranteeing by solidifying the status quo. In this connection, however, it is worth noting that one of our respondents reported a unique contract agreement between the professoriat and the institution—a college that until recently used apprentices. The new contract actually *forbids* autonomous teaching by graduate students or anyone else except the regular full-time staff! It is obvious that this faculty has come to recognize the link between exploitation of apprentices and job security.

If, as E. D. Hirsch and others have suggested, the professoriat were to return to teaching basic courses, would there be an easing of the dilemma of large numbers of teaching apprentices? One reply to our question is that for reasons of budgetary compensation there would *not* be more permanent jobs created but simply more elective courses dropped from the departmental offering. It has also been suggested that if graduate students, even in small numbers, were assisting professors but not teaching their own courses, the institution could not afford to support them with tuition exemptions and fellowships or other stipends. Although this second objection seems more serious to us than the first, the fact remains that under the present system apprentices are still their own worst enemy.

Another danger in the employment of large numbers of teaching apprentices is that the world beyond the walls of academia will find it increasingly objectionable, especially as tuition costs soar and state legislatures or trustees peruse operating budgets. For different reasons, parents, legislators, trustees, and undergraduates themselves all tend to believe that there ought to be a professor, not a graduate student, in front of the classroom. That the graduate student is saving everyone a good deal of money does not seem to modify this strong feeling. Of course not every veteran professor is necessarily a gifted pedagogue, and some apprentices are remarkably precocious as budding teachers, but there can be no substitute for knowledge and experience or for the prestige derived from distinguished teaching and scholarship. In any event, given the persistent feeling that professors do not give sufficient time to students, it is undoubtedly true that many a legislator or trustee would feel better about loosening the purse strings, or setting about to fatten the purse, were he or she assured that the veteran faculty were prepared to descend into the trenches. In this regard, the actions taken recently by the Texas State Legislature to regulate teaching loads of senior faculty and teaching apprentices may well be emulated soon in other states and by other governing authorities.

We have come to the conclusion that senior faculty have a responsibility to train their students themselves. This means that they must train teachers as well as scholars. Ideally, the senior faculty should be master teachers assisted by, and genuinely responsible for, real apprentices. But as realists we have assumed in the following recommendations the continuation of the more widespread situation of autonomous teaching by apprentices. In either case, as one of our respondents put it, "Teacher preparation would be immeasurably strengthened if the assessment of teaching in the profession were a more exact business than at present it manages to be."

Recommendations

1. Graduate departments of language and literature should not train more students than can eventually be employed in teaching or related professional activity. And those they train should not be exploited. We applaud those departments that have attempted to reduce the number of teaching apprentices or, at least, the number of classes taught by apprentices. At Virginia Polytechnic Institute and State University, Arthur Eastman, head of the English Department, recently succeeded in persuading university officials that apprentices were being exploited to the detriment of all concerned. The department received five new full-time positions. The potential benefits of such enlightened and forceful leadership are innumerable.

2. Those graduate students accepted for study in a department should be regarded as apprentices *to* faculty, not replacements *for* faculty. As they are novice scholars, so they should be considered novice teachers who need to be taught to perform effectively in the classroom through reading about and discussing relevant pedagogical ideas as well as through observing successful teachers and being observed themselves as part of a carefully supervised teaching experience.

3. Apprentices should acquire pedagogical knowledge and experience as part of a well-designed teaching apprentice program, including these essential ingredients:

(a) several pedagogical courses—emphasizing both theory and practical problems; for foreign language apprentices, these courses should include linguistics and recent research in pedagogy; for English, linguistics and rhetoric would be desirable additions to composition and literature pedagogy.

(b) significant preclassroom or preservice training to familiarize apprentices with class preparation, classroom techniques, course syllabi, grading, testing, curriculum planning, advising students.

(c) a graduated sequence from tutoring to observing and assisting a master teacher to some autonomous teaching (occasional and under guidance). If autonomous teaching by an apprentice in the first year of graduate study is deemed necessary, only those apprentices who have had previous teaching experience or who have undergone intensive training of the kind described above should be appointed.

(d) careful selection of apprentices: prospective teachers should be interviewed and tested for competency or potential capacity to teach basic courses.

(e) thorough evaluation and supervision by master teachers and other full-time faculty, including directors or coordinators of teaching apprentice programs; supervision includes advising, observation of teaching, and feedback on performance; evaluation includes keeping records and reports for files and dossiers.

(f) materials: the standard references and textbooks, current articles and books, sample papers, examinations and exercises; a handbook or other form of ready information to tell apprentices as much as possible what they need to know about the school, department, and conditions of apprenticeship, as well as practical tips for dealing with teaching responsibilities.

(g) aids: all our contributors report that audiovisual equipment of a sophisticated and remarkably helpful kind is now available and widely used for activities ranging from self-learning to videotaping of classroom performance; there should be a learning center or laboratory, appropriately equipped. The phenomenon of learning has been studied intensively in our time and the results cannot be ignored by those who are themselves learning to teach.

4. Teacher training activities should be an important *and* rewarded part of departmental activity; directors or coordinators of apprentice programs should receive adequate course remission and/or other forms of compensation, including research grants to study recent work on the teaching of composition, basic language and literature courses, and teaching apprentice programs at other institutions. The presence of a senior professor as head of the program would of course greatly enhance its prestige and affirm powerfully its centrality to departmental concerns, but it would also be desirable to have a program directed by a junior faculty member with intense interest or special expertise, provided the position offers possibilities of permanent employment and is not perceived as a dead end or a "chore" to be endured.

5. Departments should encourage outside evaluation of their programs. This is especially important for new and growing activities. There are many effective teaching apprentice programs, including those described in Part II, that can serve as models for, and their directors or coordinators as evaluators of, one's own departmental activity.

6. Relatively few departments have sought funding from outside sources to establish and support ongoing activities or programs, notable exceptions described above being the Exxon and Danforth Fund grants utilized in, respectively, the Cornell Summer Program and the Near Eastern Studies Program at Michigan. Given the great national interest in improving teaching, both government and private sources of such funding should be carefully explored.

7. Foundations and professional organizations interested in the teaching of language and literature should be stimulated to make available publications and materials that can be useful to apprentice programs. Individual programs or learning centers that have generated such materials could be assisted in making them available to others on an exchange basis through announcements in professional publications.

8. It is increasingly recognized that the separation of teaching and scholarship in graduate study, which was brought about by focusing entirely on literary works as objects to be studied, has been a fundamental error. This error has led to inadequate preparation for teaching literature and to the failure of graduate students to grasp any connection between their literary scholarship and the teaching of composition or basic language courses. As New York University's Paula Johnson puts it, "Graduate programs in English need to recognize that people who go through them will probably teach both literature and composition, and design the programs accordingly. Concentrations and degrees in rhetoric alone seem to me less needed than graduate programs broadly in *literacy*—taking all kinds of reading and writing into consideration." The teaching of literature should also claim equal attention with the teaching of language. Though the focus has been on English composition and basic language learning in most teaching apprentice programs, there is much

new interest in the techniques of teaching, for example, masterpieces of literature or such genres as comedy and tragedy. Since language and literature are
obviously related and apprentice teachers, it is hoped, will eventually teach
both, literary texts should be approached from a pedagogical view as part of
graduate training.

9. In this regard, it may *not* be desirable to split departmental apprentice
programs into such divisions as rhetoric, writing, and literature. No matter how
large or well-intentioned the program, apprentices should have experience in
these interrelated subjects, since it is clear that regular faculty are called on to
teach all of them.

10. Apprentices should be appropriately rewarded with tuition remission
and stipend. If, as in our ideal model, the apprentices are assistants to master
teachers, they should be paid a stipend sufficient to enable them to support
themselves while studying. Where there is autonomous teaching, the apprentice should be paid a sum roughly equivalent to the amount a beginning
assistant professor might be paid for teaching a similar course.

11. More attention should be given to the possibility of internships. Although intraschool arrangements exist, they are relatively rare. Of special importance would be arrangements between two- and four-year institutions that
do not have graduate programs and those universities that have graduate
departments and teaching apprentice programs.

12. The participation of apprentices in departmental governance raises
interesting questions because of the special status of such students as faculty-
in-training. We recommend that as a minimum there be provision for participation of apprentices in all matters affecting their work, that is, curriculum,
textbooks, testing, and administration of the program itself.

13. To minimize exploitation and assure that apprentices get on with their
doctoral studies, there should be a limit on the number of years an apprentice
can be employed. We think that a total of two or three years for combined
M.A. and Ph.D. study is an appropriate limit, especially if teaching duties have
clearly delayed progress toward the degree.

14. Despite the existence of various forms of "buddying" in current programs, more can be done to ensure that the teaching apprentice enjoys the
benefits of sharing the experience with fellow apprentices. For example, apprentices should be urged to work together on materials, to exchange valuable
practical experiences, to visit one another's classrooms; more advanced apprentices can naturally take the lead in organizing and directing such consultations
and exchanges.

15. For the benefit of apprentices, as well as regular faculty, there should
be a planned departmental series of lectures, demonstrations, symposia, and
panels featuring, but not limited to, especially outstanding visiting authorities;
while auto-contemplation of one's own program can be limiting, highlighting
or advertising to internal audiences the accomplishments of a program can
be both stimulating and justifying.

16. Departments should express their support for teaching apprentice programs loudly and clearly. This can be done by the establishment of interdepartmental teaching apprentice committees charged with stimulating and
coordinating the activities of individual departmental programs and by active
involvement of the entire professoriat in the actual daily routines of teacher
training.

17. Finally, teacher training should be an institutional priority. When there is a university-wide program, such as the Danforth Foundation–sponsored project at Harvard or the Teaching Improvement Program of the State University of New York, there is a greater commitment of energy and funds, more likelihood of cooperation among departments, and greater external interest than there is with an individual department effort.

If, in reviewing the complete results of our study, we had to select a single comment that would sum up the state of teaching apprentice activities in language and literature in the United States and Canada at the present time, it would probably be the remarks with which Woodruff C. Thomson, Coordinator of Composition in Brigham Young University's Department of English, concluded his response:

> Teacher preparation is improving. This I sense as I attend professional meetings and conferences. And it should improve. After all, we are training *professionals*. Why shouldn't our "products" be given as careful training and preparation as a budding lawyer or an M.B.A. student?

In short, teacher training in language and literature departments has enjoyed considerable progress over the past several years, but our profession's journey to excellence in this area is far from complete.

PART TWO: SELECTED PROGRAM DESCRIPTIONS

University of Arkansas, Department of Foreign Languages

James F. Ford, Renate A. Schulz, and Margaret Clark

History of the Program

Graduate programs in modern foreign languages at the University of Arkansas date back to 1950, when the M.A. degree in German began to be offered. Separate departments existed for Classics, German, and Romance languages. In 1955 the M.A. degree in French was initiated, followed by Spanish in 1957. In 1965 the three departments merged to form the present Department of Foreign Languages. Teaching assistants were used on a limited basis from the inception of the graduate programs, and the number increased substantially during the latter half of the sixties, when the foreign language requirement in the College of Arts and Sciences was increased to twelve semester hours. During this period the practice of using graduate students to teach sections of elementary language was established. Until the early seventies, coordination of the elementary language programs and supervision of the teaching assistants was performed by members of the department whose specialties, background, and experience were not necessarily suited to the task. This pattern continued into the early seventies, when the department recognized a need for foreign language education specialists; a specialist was added in French in 1972, in Spanish in 1974, and in German in 1977.

Objectives and Purposes of the Program

Currently the Department of Foreign Languages offers the M.A. degree in French, German, and Spanish and contributes in varying degrees to the M.A. and Ph.D. in Comparative Literature and the M.F.A. in Translation, housed in the Department of English. The purpose of the assistantship is, in part, to support graduate work in these areas. Most of our graduates, however, enter the teaching profession (usually at the secondary level), and we recognize that the apprentice teaching experience is one of the most vital components of their graduate training.

Organization of the Program

Since the administration expects that the majority of our elementary service courses to be taught by graduate teaching assistants, funding for the TA program is based on projected enrollment and the number of service courses to be offered. Currently the college requires six semester hours of foreign language study (reduced in 1971), which most students satisfy by completing a two-course elementary sequence in French, German, or Spanish. Over the last several years, we have supported an average of twenty-three graduate assistants per year (8 in French, 5 in German, 10 in Spanish). The numbers in each language are distributed according to our instructional needs in each elementary program.

Functioning of the Program

Selection procedures. A departmental committee representing the three languages reviews the applications and recommends to the chairman of the department those students to whom financial assistance should be offered. Criteria for selection include those specified for admission to the Graduate School (bachelor's degree or equivalent with a 2.5 grade-point average; 4.0 = A). The department further takes into consideration the extent and quality of undergraduate language study, evidence of oral proficiency in the language, experience abroad, and prior teaching experience.

Preteaching orientation. Beginning in 1977 all new teaching assistants were required by university mandate to attend a one-week workshop before the beginning of fall classes. This workshop has been conducted primarily by the College of Education; however, those departments that are interested in training their own assistants have asked that new TAs spend part of the week in their home department. We were given two days in 1978 and three days in 1979 for a departmental orientation. Since the fall of 1980, TAs for foreign languages have spent the entire week in a departmental preservice workshop. The workshop is conducted primarily by the three foreign language education specialists on our staff.

Concurrent methods course. From 1974 until 1978, all new teaching assistants were required by the department to enroll in a language-specific practicum course that was taught by each specialist for his or her group. In 1978 we decided to move to a departmental practicum (internship), designed and taught by one of our specialists and focusing on basic methodological concepts and their practical application to elementary foreign language instruction. This course serves as an in-depth continuation of the initial preservice workshop experience. In addition to topics on teaching and testing the four skills (listening, reading comprehension, speaking, and writing) and such related areas as culture, the course introduces the assistants to some of the basic resources in foreign language education and attempts to instill a sense of professionalism. The course carries three semester hours of graduate credit and meets for two hours per week, with one additional meeting conducted by the respective language supervisor to discuss specific day-to-day problems in the elementary courses and to plan and write departmental tests and examinations.

Duties and responsibilities of the TA. Teaching assistants are normally assigned six semester hours of teaching duties, arranged as two three-hour elementary courses or one elementary course and three basic conversation courses (one-credit-hour supplementary courses that are designed for the more highly motivated beginning language students). In addition, each TA is required to schedule three hours per week for student conferences. Tentative teaching assignments are made at the end of the orientation workshop, but they may be adjusted after fall registration is completed. Teaching materials, including textbooks, workbooks, detailed course descriptions, and daily class plans, are provided by the supervisor, and a variety of audiovisual materials (both hardware and software) is also available through the department. Additionally, the department has prepared a "Handbook for Teaching Assistants," which outlines duties and responsibilities as well as departmental policies and administrative procedures as they relate to the organization and instruction of multiple-section elementary language courses.

Supervision. Over the years the department has experimented with various models of supervision. During 1978–79 each new teaching assistant who had little or no teaching experience was assigned to at least one elementary section under the direct supervision of a full-time faculty member. This arrangement was intended to provide several advantages to TAs: (1) opportunities for observing and teaching under an experienced teacher, (2) supervised planning, and (3) frequent observations and day-to-day guidance by the cooperating professor. Further, this one-to-one pairing of a TA with a regular faculty member was to ensure more direct involvement of full-time faculty in the elementary programs. During the course of the year, however, certain problems emerged that caused us to rethink this supervisory arrangement. Among them were: (1) a lack of common criteria for evaluating teaching, (2) differences in teaching style and philosophy between the specialist-supervisor and the cooperating professor, (3) difficulties for TAs in determining lines of responsibility and authority, and (4) widely varying degrees of commitment and cooperation on the part of the faculty. While we have not totally abandoned the concept of the "cooperating professor," it has been temporarily shelved, primarily because of a staffing shortage within the department. Currently, the coordination and supervision of the multiple-section elementary courses are handled again exclusively by the three foreign language education specialists. The respective supervisor visits each teaching assistant a minimum of three times per semester, beginning generally some three weeks after the beginning of classes. When TAs have an inordinate number of problems, the number of visits increases. During each visit the supervisor completes an observation report and schedules a conference with the TA to discuss the visit. During the conference, both positive and negative aspects of the TA's performance are discussed. The three supervisors occasionally cross-visit, and all full-time faculty in the three language areas are encouraged to visit the TA's classes and make formal observation reports. The criteria used for evaluation serve to apprise both the TA and the faculty as to what aspects of classroom behavior are considered important. Additionally, the supervisors and other faculty who have observed TAs are asked to complete an "End of Semester Evaluation" form. This assessment, along with pertinent factors, such as student evaluations and academic performance, is used to determine whether the assistantship will be renewed. At midterm, students in the elementary sections are asked to complete a one-page evaluation, which is seen and used only by the TA. At the end of the semester, the students are asked to complete a more extensive evaluation of the course and the instructor. This evaluation not only serves the department as an indication of student perception of the TA but also helps in evaluating course structure, materials, examinations, and so on. To recognize, encourage, and reward good teaching by TAs, the department has, since

1980–81, given an annual award to a TA judged to have performed outstand-
ingly in his or her teaching duties. The department also now requests regular
evaluations of supervisors and of the TA training provided.

While it is the prerogative of the chairman to reduce the teaching loads of
the supervisors, this action would mean a reduction in the number of courses
the department could offer, which would, in turn, reduce the overall foreign
language enrollment. Since our budgetary allotment is predicated largely on
enrollment, the elementary supervisors have agreed to perform these functions
as an overload.

Employment status of teaching assistants. On selection, the TA candidate
is sent a letter of offer that stipulates the teaching duties, graduate study
obligations, and the stipend. The letter also stipulates the conditions for reappointment: a 3.0 grade-point average and satisfactory performance of teaching
duties. While theoretically appointments are made on an annual basis, the
department reserves the right to terminate a TA at the end of any semester
in which performance has been unsatisfactory. The first semester is viewed as
largely probationary. Unsatisfactory performance in either academic work or
teaching responsibilities is reported to the chairman of the department, who
then reviews the case with the Graduate Student Committee. Depending on
the nature of the case, the committee may decide to continue the appointment
for an additional probationary semester or the TA may be dismissed. If a
student maintains the minimally acceptable grade-point average and performs
the assigned teaching duties to the satisfaction of the supervisor, the assistantship is automatically renewable for the subsequent term. University Graduate
School regulations limit financial support for students pursuing a master's degree to four semesters and for those pursuing post-master's degrees to eight.

Graduate student grievances that cannot be settled at the faculty level may
be brought to the attention of the chairman of the department. The chairman
then calls a meeting of the Graduate Student Committee, which decides
whether the case warrants a hearing. If a hearing is called, the graduate
student and any faculty who may be involved are given an opportunity to
present their respective cases. After this procedure, the committee in consultation with the chairman makes a ruling, which is communicated to the graduate
student. A student who feels that ruling is not satisfactory may appeal to the
graduate dean.

Inasmuch as most of our graduate students remain with us for only four
semesters, hold half-time teaching assignments, and carry nine semester hours
of course work each semester, we do not feel that the department would
benefit from their involvement in departmental governance.

Current Problems and Difficulties Encountered in Achieving Goals

Insufficient number of qualified applicants. Because virtually all our basic
language courses are taught by TAs, it is extremely important to us that these
courses be taught by individuals who have excellent language fluency and can
inspire, motivate, and encourage continued foreign language study. Because of
the low priority of foreign language study in Arkansas postsecondary institutions (from which we draw most applicants), only a small pool of applicants is
available. The problem is further compounded by the low TA stipends, which
are not competitive with those offered by other area institutions. We have seen

TAs with double majors resign their appointments within weeks of the start of the fall semester because they received more lucrative offers from other colleges or departments within the university.

Lack of administrative and financial support. Although our specialists fulfill the threefold role of TA trainers, supervisors, and multisection-course coordinators, they receive neither released time nor extra remuneration for their supervisory or coordinating duties. These functions are performed as an overload.

Time constraints. Insufficient time is available for individual classroom observations and conferences, which are particularly important for new TAs during the first few weeks of a semester. Because the supervisors have heavy teaching loads or administrative duties, TAs do not receive the optimum amount of assistance in developing a teaching style.

Future Plans and Prospects

From a self-evaluation completed by the department in 1979, the following priorities concerning staffing and supervision of the elementary programs have been established:

Improving screening of TA applicants through in-person or telephone interviews and/or tape recordings to ensure applicants' language fluency.

Obtaining released time or course-load reductions for supervisors to enable them to provide improved individual guidance to new TAs.

Seeking funding to hire fully qualified instructors in order to reduce dependence on TAs for teaching elementary courses and in order to reduce class size.

Seeking funding to increase TA stipends in order to be more competitive within the region and to attract high-quality applicants for our graduate programs.

Developing a program for self-critique and self-evaluation by increasing the use of videotape and audiotape recordings.

Instituting a one-semester training and observation period for new TAs so that first-time teaching and first-semester graduate study do not coincide. During this period TAs would receive formal instruction in foreign language pedagogy, have opportunities for classroom observations, assist in preparing teaching materials, construct and grade oral and written tests, supervise and monitor the language laboratory, and provide tutorial assistance to students who experience language-learning difficulties.

Including pedagogical training and experience in the required core offerings for the M.A. degree: since the department has a strong pedagogical emphasis and since most of our M.A. graduates become teachers in secondary schools or community colleges, all M.A. candidates would be required to take one course in psycholinguistics or foreign language pedagogy and to gain some limited classroom experience. This degree requirement would also be reflected in the M.A. reading list (by including pedagogically oriented sources and references) as well as in the M.A. comprehensive examinations (by including one or more pedagogically oriented questions).

Increasing offerings of pedagogically oriented courses to provide a minor field of concentration for those candidates with special interests in foreign language teaching.

University of California, Berkeley, Department of Comparative Literature

Janette Richardson

The Department of Comparative Literature at Berkeley has offered a freshman reading and composition course since the inception of the department in 1964. This course is the only one for which graduate students are customarily employed—either as "associates" or "acting instructors," who are responsible for individual sections of the course, or as "teaching assistants," who work with the instructors and conduct additional tutorial sessions. Originally, the operation was small and TAs received the pedagogical assistance deemed necessary from the regular faculty members teaching the course, but by 1967 it became obvious that this informal method was no longer adequate. Because the course satisfies a requirement of the College of Letters and Science, the number of sections offered had increased so much that advanced graduate students were needed to do at least part of the regular teaching; and because of the diverse nature of comparative literature, many prospectively excellent instructors were foreign language majors who had had minimal exposure to English composition in their own academic training. The department, therefore, instituted a one-unit course (i.e., meeting once a week) on the teaching of English composition in connection with the reading of masterpieces of world literature and required that all newly appointed TAs register for it. An expanded version of this course is still in operation.

At present, the department employs a limited number of TAs, who are selected by a committee of graduate faculty members from among applicants who have completed the M.A. degree and received permission to proceed to the Ph.D. It employs a large number of associates and acting instructors, customarily drawn by the committee from the ranks of the departmental TAs. In addition to the eligibility requirements for the TAs, associates must have one year of teaching experience; acting instructors must have passed the Ph.D. Qualifying Examinations and have two years of teaching experience. Funding for TAs is part of the regular departmental budget, and thus the number of positions does not vary from year to year; associates and acting instructors are paid from temporary funds allotted to the department by the College of Letters and Science, and their number depends on yearly student enrollments. There is a four-year limit on such employment, but the successful TA may expect to be advanced within this time frame to the actual teaching positions of associate and acting instructor as long as progress toward the Ph.D. is satisfactory. All levels of appointments are usually three-quarter contracts, associates and acting instructors teaching one section of the freshman course each quarter of the regular academic year (exclusive of summer session) and TAs participating in only two sections over the three-quarter span. Acting instructors and associates have full responsibility for their sections, including selecting the assigned literary texts (within the framework of certain departmental guidelines), organizing the course, devising writing assignments, awarding final grades, and, if they have a full section (i.e., 30 students with a

TA), directing the work of the assistant. TAs evaluate three-fourths of the papers written, conduct two tutorial sections per week devoted to effective composition and supplementary analysis of the literary works being studied, and hold individual conferences (as do the associates and acting instructors) with students who need extra help. Thus, it is obvious that Ph.D. students who are involved in this apprentice program have ample opportunity to develop pedagogic skills for undergraduate instruction.

Their training course, which is conducted by a senior faculty member, until 1978 focused on methods for teaching English composition, since it was assumed that graduate students in literature had sufficient chance to observe effective teaching of literary works in their own classes and in the sections of the freshman course for which they served as TAs. Associates and acting instructors, however, intermittently expressed interest in having some sort of colloquium addressed to their situation as beginning teachers of literature, so the training program was expanded to its present form. Beginning TAs are still required to enroll for the course on teaching composition, which runs simultaneously with their first employment experience, but they may also take part, if they wish, in a second series of weekly meetings, on the teaching of both literature and composition, that are organized for associates and acting instructors. The former course concentrates on the evaluation of student writing and on methods for instilling better understanding of effective use of language, for generating thesis ideas in relation to literary analysis, and for expounding adequate evidence to support such theses. This course is conducted in the fall quarter, and the TAs are asked to submit at the end of the course a few Xerox copies of student papers they have evaluated. In the subsequent quarter the professor visits tutorial sections conducted by the TAs and then confers with each assistant about strengths and weaknesses observed in both classroom technique and paper evaluation. Since students at Berkeley regularly evaluate instructors and TAs in the courses they have completed, this information is also discussed in the conference between professor and TA. In addition, TAs are encouraged to bring any special problems they may encounter to the professor for private discussion or for inclusion in the class meetings.

The weekly sessions for associates and acting instructors, which have been organized by a senior acting instructor specially hired to work with the professor who conducts the course for TAs, have a variable format that is determined by the interest or need of the participants. Various faculty specialists have talked to the group about teaching the different literary genres included in the freshman course or about other writing programs on campus. Individual participants have given demonstrations of their methods for tackling common problems. They have worked out a system for visiting one another's classes and talking together about their mutual evaluations. Perhaps most valuable of all, they have developed a resource center for teachers of the freshman course that includes a variety of books on English composition, texts of the literary works most frequently taught and some of the better relevant criticism, a collection of slides that may be used to supplement the teaching of those works, and a file of paper topics and other assignments that the donors have thought particularly successful. The truly remarkable things about this aspect of the apprentice program are its voluntary nature and the heightened awareness of, and seriousness about, effective teaching that have resulted from peer cooperation.

Perhaps a third of the comparative literature graduate students work in the freshman course and thus participate in the training program, and this selectivity is a problem that has not been solved. It is true that many other comparative literature students are employed by other departments, mostly foreign languages, and receive pedagogic training there, but too many do not get the opportunity to teach before they complete their degrees. Another potential problem is the minimal supervision built into the program, but as long as a senior faculty member is willing to direct the operation instead of teaching only his or her specialty, it is unlikely that the department will do as some others at Berkeley have and hire someone exclusively for such supervision and training. The present system is reasonably successful.

University of California, Davis, Department of Spanish and Classics

Fabián A. Samaniego

Before 1970, teaching assistants in the Department of Spanish and Classics at the University of California at Davis (UCD) were supervised by two or three professors on a rotating basis. The supervision generally consisted of preparing a syllabus for the beginning and intermediate courses and visiting each TA's class once or twice a year. The training typically consisted of telling the TAs one or two days before classes began what classes they would be teaching, handing them a syllabus, and sending them into the classroom.

Because of widespread student dissatisfaction with elementary foreign language courses and, more specifically, with the foreign language requirement, a well-organized student movement succeeded in 1970 in eliminating the foreign language requirement at eight of the nine University of California campuses. Only Davis retained the foreign language requirement, which dropped from eighteen to twelve units. In a conscious effort to improve the quality of the remaining required courses, the Department of Spanish and Classics hired a full-time TA supervisor with sole responsibility for training and supervising TAs and for coordinating and supervising the elementary and intermediate language courses.

Thus, my first few years at UCD were dedicated to phasing out the eighteen-unit program and phasing in the new twelve-unit program. Because continuing TAs in the department were accustomed to working on their own, I decided to limit my work with them to that of a full-time consultant and troubleshooter and to concentrate my effort on the new TAs.

As long as student and TA complaints were kept to a minimum, the Spanish Department gave me a free hand in setting up a supervisory program. No departmental committee was assigned to oversee the work; I was responsible directly to the chairperson. This practice has had a very favorable effect on the program.

The program has two principal objectives: to provide quality teaching to students enrolled in courses taught by TAs and to produce quality teachers skilled in varied subject matter, teaching methods, and evaluation procedures and capable of evaluating their own teaching effectiveness. Because the faculty feel that TA supervision should be done by the person specifically hired and trained for this position and because the TAs prefer to be responsible to only one person, faculty members other than the TA supervisor are not involved in the program.

Funding for TA training and supervision is available both from departmental funds and from the University through undergraduate instructional improvement grants. These grants have been a major source of funds for developing various types of teaching aids, such as slide/sound culture units and videotape presentations of particularly difficult grammatical structures. Funding from these grants has also been used to develop new course options, such as our Individualized Elementary Spanish Program, which in turn provide additional teaching training and experience.

The TA training and supervision program consists of several preteaching orientation and training sessions, two required methods courses, ongoing supervision and evaluation through both classroom visitations and video feedback, and a rotation system designed to allow TAs to get varied teaching experience.

The preteaching orientation and training are done the week before classes begin by the TA supervisor together with personnel from UCD's Teaching Resources Center (T.R.C.). The center conducts a four- to six-hour orientation session for all new foreign language TAs; these sessions are carefully planned in close consultation with the foreign language TA supervisors to ensure that the training meets both the general needs of the university and the more specific needs of the individual departments. General orientation information includes topics such as "The Role of the TA on the UCD Campus" and "Teaching Resources Available on the UCD Campus," and more specific topics may be "What to Do the First Day of Class" and "A Fears and Trauma Question/Answer Session Conducted by Experienced Foreign Language TAs." In addition to the T.R.C. orientation, new TAs in the Spanish Department spend a couple of days with the TA supervisor going over specifics of the courses they will be teaching—textbooks, teaching methods, pacing, language lab procedures, testing and grading. Continuing TAs and "associates in teaching" also meet with the TA supervisor at the beginning of each quarter to review the specifics of the courses they will be teaching. Generally, two hour meetings are set up with all Spanish I TAs, all Spanish II TAs, and all Spanish III TAs. Additional sessions are then scheduled for all new TAs.

TAs and associates in teaching are selected by members of the Graduate Admissions and TA Selection Committee. Selection is based entirely on academic promise. All TAs are required to enroll in Spanish 390A and 390B, Teaching College Spanish, during their first fall and spring quarters at UCD. Spanish 390A is a three-unit methods course that meets three hours a week. Approximately one of the three hours is spent reviewing the particular material that is to be taught by the TAs that week, anticipating problems that are likely to arise in class and answering any questions the TAs may have regarding grammar and/or procedure. The remaining two hours are spent discussing teaching theory. The assigned texts for the methods course are Frank Grittner's *Teaching Foreign Languages* (2nd ed., New York: Harper and Row, 1977) and Beverly Galyean's *Language from Within* (Santa Barbara, Calif.: Confluent Education Development and Research Center, 1976).

The methods class covers such topics as the reasons for studying a foreign language, pattern practice techniques, affective activities, the language lab, testing and evaluation, individualized instruction, teaching aids, teaching reading and writing, selection of textbooks, and bilingual education. A deliberate effort is made to give this course a practical orientation; for example, the Spanish 390A syllabus is coordinated with the Spanish I syllabus so that when the TAs begin to use pattern drills in class, pattern drill techniques will have just been discussed in the methods class. When the TAs must prepare their first class quiz, testing and grading will have already been discussed in the methods class. This immediate application of what is being learned not only motivates TAs to do their best but also helps them develop self-confidence and good teaching habits from the start.

In the Spanish 390A course the TAs must complete three projects, each of which is designed to have the TAs learn by doing. These projects are closely tied to the topics being presented in the methods class and include such assignments as "develop a slide/sound culture unit for use in your Spanish I class" or "demonstrate you understand the concepts of individualization by individualizing a lesson in a given textbook" or "teach six hours in the UCD individualized program." TAs are also given the option of suggesting their own projects; several of these projects have been published.

Spanish 390B is a one-unit problems course to be taken when a TA teaches Spanish II for the first time. In 390B, as in 390A, the TA supervisor tries to help the TAs anticipate problems in teaching the specific material of Spanish II. The class meets one hour a week, but, unlike Spanish 390A, it is graded simply as pass/no pass.

It is worth noting that when the Spanish 390 course was proposed, the department, which places a strong emphasis on literature in its graduate program, approved it as a requirement for all new TAs but would not allow it to count toward the units required for the M.A. degree. As a result, beginning TAs were forced to take their heaviest course load (two graduate seminars and Spanish 390) during their first quarter in graduate school and, for most, during the first experience teaching a course. It wasn't long before the TAs organized themselves and demanded that the 390 course be given graduate-seminar status and count not only as one of the two courses they were required to take as TAs but also as credit toward the M.A. degree. Both demands were met.

TAs in our department teach the first-year courses, Spanish I, II, III, and/or the parallel Individualized Elementary Spanish 1AT, 2AT, 3AT (AT = autotutorial). A rotation system is set up requiring that all TAs start their teaching with Spanish I and teach each level course two consecutive quarters before being assigned the next level course. We have found that repeating each course before moving on to the next has helped considerably in building up the TAs' self-confidence and in eliminating the element of surprise in teaching assignments. TAs are not rotated into the individualized program until after they have taught both Spanish I and II because in the AT program instructors may be faced with teaching Spanish I, II, and III all within the same hour. Also, since the individualized and the lockstep programs use the same textbook, it is important that AT instructors be familiar with most if not all of the text before teaching in the AT program.

Courses beyond the first year are taught by third- and fourth-year graduate students. These students generally hold the title "associate in teaching" and usually teach Spanish 4, a five-unit grammar review course, or Spanish 5 and 6, two three-unit grammar review and reading courses. They may also be assigned to teach several of the two-unit conversation courses, Spanish 8A, 8B, or 9. Our failure to supervise apprentices assigned to teach Spanish 4-9 is a weakness in our program which resulted from the rapid growth of our individualized elementary Spanish courses. (Approximately 350–400 students per quarter enroll in the lockstep Spanish 1-3 courses and another 350–400 students enroll in the individualized courses.) The increase in enrollment almost doubled the TA supervisor's duties and responsibilities at the first-year level, making it necessary to relieve him of responsibility for the second-year courses.

In all courses, Spanish 1-9, the TA or the associate in teaching is the sole instructor of the class he or she teaches. In the first-year courses the TA supervisor prepares the course syllabus and oversees the testing and grading procedures, but only the TA can assign the students' final course grades since it is the TA who is in daily contact with the students. TAs prepare and grade their own quizzes. All TAs teaching the same level course help to prepare and grade the midterm and final exams. In Spanish 1-3, 25% of the student's final course grade is based on the TA's subjective evaluation of the student's daily class participation.

A conscious effort to create an atmosphere of trust and openness is made throughout a TA's apprenticeship at UCD. Repeatedly the TAs are reminded that their supervisor is not an evaluator but rather a helper, a resource person, a troubleshooter, a teacher trainer. They are made aware that it is normal and even expected that they will have problems with their teaching and that they should not be embarrassed to ask for help. The questions they ask may vary from "What is a direct object?" and "How do you explain preterite versus imperfect?" to "How do you help a failing student?" and "How do I know how many points to assign each part of my quizzes?" Simple as many of these questions may be, it is extremely important that the TAs have confidence to ask their questions. If the TAs know that they are not expected to be perfect and that they may ask for help when they need it, the program has attained two specific goals.

Besides maintaining an informal, open-door policy with the TAs, encouraging them to seek advice any time they have a problem, we follow a rather formal classroom visitation procedure. The TA supervisor is the only faculty member who visits TAs' classes. TAs are usually visited twice each quarter during their first two quarters at UCD. After that, except when TAs have particular problems, their classes are visited once a quarter. When visiting classes the supervisor stays the whole hour and holds a half- to one-hour conference with the TA later that day or the following day. Usually the conference begins with the supervisor asking the TA if the class observed was typical or atypical and why. Then the TA is asked what he or she particularly liked about how the class was conducted. The answer allows the supervisor to comment on the strong features of the TA's presentation. They then talk about what the TA did not like about the class and focus on those things that should be improved. If a TA has problems, such as using too much English, giving unclear explanations, using poor drilling techniques, and so on, these problems can be focused on and made the specific goal for the week. The supervisor then tries to visit the class again within a week or two.

Recently the TAs' classes were videotaped and followed up with a one-hour, three-person video-playback session where the TA, the video-feedback analyst from the Teaching Resources Center, and the supervisor viewed and evaluated the taped class. This procedure has added entirely new dimensions to the traditional classroom visits. With videotape, discussion about the class gets completely away from comments such as "Remember when you were doing the exercise on . . . ?" and focuses instead on a class that is in progress. The TA is much quicker to recognize such problems as overuse of English, unclear grammatical explanations, too much writing on the board, lack of variety in class activity, and so on. Having the T.R.C. video-feedback analyst present adds greater objectivity and helps ensure that emphasis is placed not only on problem solving and dealing with particular methods or subjects but also on developing each TA as a confident new teacher.

The Spanish Department has not required that written reports on the TA's teaching effectiveness be submitted; therefore this practice has not been followed in the past. An evaluation form is completed after each class visit or video-feedback session and is kept on file. These forms are used solely by the supervisor to help keep track of an individual TA's progress and problems.

TAs and associates in teaching in our department receive one-year contracts for $6,273 and $6,354 respectively. These are automatically renewable for a second year for M.A. candidates and for up to four years for Ph.D. candidates, provided academic standards are maintained. When poor teaching has made it necessary to reconsider renewal of an individual's teaching assistantship, the department has repeatedly voted to discontinue those TAs who were also doing poor work in their graduate seminars and invariably has voted to continue to support those who were doing good work in their academic courses. Thus, teaching quality has not played a significant role in the decision to renew a teaching assistantship. There is no formal grievance procedure established should an individual wish to take issue with a departmental decision.

Graduate students in our department have the right to elect two representatives who may attend departmental faculty meetings as nonvoting members. In addition, one or two graduate student members may be appointed to the departmental standing committees.

Problems and difficulties in achieving the goals of this TA training program have centered on a lack of recognition, by the Spanish Department faculty, of the importance of quality teaching and on a reluctance to allow both TAs and the TA supervisor the time necessary to develop good teaching skills. The Spanish Department at UCD is not unlike most other foreign language departments. Most of the faculty are highly specialized in literature, and although they recognize a need for TA supervision, they have difficulty giving it too much importance. After all, most of them served their teaching apprenticeship with little or no supervision, and, of course, all of them were highly successful at it! Suddenly to have to replace one graduate seminar with a methods class is far beyond the comprehension of many, if not most, of our colleagues in literature, and to admit that a good potential scholar in Spanish or Spanish-American literature may not be a good teacher of elementary Spanish is totally unacceptable. As a result, the TAs have had to demand recognition of the importance of TA training, and the TA supervisor has had to constantly justify the need for a lighter teaching load in order to have time for supervision.

One way to partially solve these problems is to involve more faculty in the actual supervision of TAs. Involvement creates a more realistic awareness of the problems brought about by poor teaching and, therefore, of the need for, and importance of, quality TA training and supervison. In an effort to move toward more active faculty involvement in TA supervision, a committee is currently working on developing a departmental TA teaching evaluation form to be filled out by the TA supervisor in consultation with individual TAs after each class visit. The forms will be made available to the faculty when reappointment of TAs is being considered. It is hoped that this procedure will not only begin to involve faculty in TA supervision but also serve to make them more aware of TA teaching quality in the department.

Colorado State University, Department of English

James E. Tanner

This essay describes six aspects of the apprentice program currently in effect for M.A. candidates awarded Teaching Assistantships in Composition at Colorado State University: background, objectives, policies and procedures, courses, staffing and funding, and prospects.

Background

The English Department of Colorado State University (CSU)—a land-grant institution with an enrollment of 18,000—has offered the M.A. for twenty-three years and, during that period, has always appointed Graduate Teaching Assistants in Composition. CSU has an all-university composition requirement, and our twenty-eight GTAs carry at least half of the resulting teaching load. Our regular faculty of forty carry the other half, with every faculty member teaching a section of composition each semester. Until 1979–80 we required of all undergraduates a two-semester sequence of composition courses, with GTAs teaching the first course and faculty the second.

Serious training of GTAs has been long in coming. In the 1950s they received no formal training; the 1960s saw presession orientations and a course syllabus. In the 1970s we began to require that GTAs take a course in composition analysis during their first semester of teaching, and we began to supervise their entire period of service. A Professional Internship in English (PIE) program and an associated course requirement form the core of the present teaching apprentice program.

The program was, of necessity, severely understaffed and consequently unevenly administered through most of the 1970s. Eventually the same circumstances that caused this staffing shortage forced a revision of our entire composition program. A steady dwindling of resources, a mounting backlog of students needing composition courses, and department dissatisfaction with training and teaching efforts led us to abandon our two-course composition requirement in 1979. A new composition program went into effect with the following components:

A comprehensive placement program. Each incoming student is required to take a 1½-hour essay exam that is holistically scored on a nine-point scale by English Department faculty. This score is combined with the student's verbal SAT or ACT score and high school English GPA to arrive at a composite placement score. All students are then ranked on the basis of their scores and placed in one of three categories.

A Composition Fundamentals course (CO101). The course, required of all students with low placement scores, normally enrolls fifteen to twenty percent of the student body.

A College Writing course (CO150). All nonexempted CSU students must take this course to satisfy the all-university composition requirement.

An exempt-with-credit status (CO150T) for the six to eight percent of students with high placement.

A comprehensive training program for GTAs.

In anticipation of adopting a new program the department replaced two retiring faculty with composition specialists and expanded administrative and supervisory staffing for composition. We decided, for a long list of reasons, to give half of our new CO150 sections to GTAs and the other half to faculty rather than put faculty members in charge of all sections and assign GTAs as genuine assistants. Extensive GTA training was included in the new program because a GTA-taught writing course would be the only exposure to the English Department that many students would get and because the level of preparation we could expect of new graduate students had dropped to the point where we could no longer assume they knew even "the basics."

Objectives

Our goals in the new Professional Internship in English (PIE) training program are simple. We want to ensure that CSU students receive from English Department GTAs instruction that is of uniformly high quality. We also want to provide GTAs with thorough training in the theory and practice of teaching expository writing at the college level, to help GTAs become competitive on the current academic job market, and to encourage the productive exchange of ideas among our GTAs and regular faculty about the teaching of composition.

Policies and Procedures

Eligibility. Graduate students may enter the PIE program in their first year; normally they apply for an assistantship when requesting admission to one of our graduate programs. Our graduate students in literature, creative writing, communications development, and TEFL/linguistics are all eligible for Graduate Teaching Assistantships in Composition.

Selection. GTA applicants are first screened by one of four faculty subcommittees (in the candidates' academic areas of specialization) and ranked on the basis of academic potential. Then all applications are combined and ranked for teaching potential by faculty composition specialists. Both rankings are based on undergraduate record, letters, a writing sample, and optional GRE scores. The Graduate Coordinator and the Director of Composition then combine the rankings, juggling various interests to produce a pool of acceptable GTA candidates that promises balance among the four academic concentrations; money for the most promising students; good teachers in the composition classrooms; a sufficient number to fill available slots; a fair representation of ages, sexes, and races; and professional survival for the administrators concerned. Offers are then made until slots are filled or the pool is emptied.

Orientation and Training. Preliminaries. In early summer new GTAs are sent texts and syllabi for fall classes, an orientation schedule, a contract, and various instructions and reassurances. They are also required to attend two weeks of intensive orientation before classes start. The orientation focuses on basic writers and their problems; it prepares GTAs for the Composition Fundamentals class they teach in their first semester. Materials used in CO101 are distributed and explained, and GTAs are introduced to the resources of the department's composition library (texts, tests, exercises, writing samples).

First-semester training. New GTAs each teach one section of CO101, Composition Fundamentals. They must also enroll in a methods course—E684, Supervised College Teaching, which is taught by a faculty composition specialist. E684 is both a prior and a concurrent course; GTAs receive instruction and supervision in the teaching of CO101 and preview the course they will add to their teaching schedules in subsequent semesters—CO150, College Writing. In their first semester of E684 GTAs study the required CO150 texts and syllabus and learn techniques for teaching this material. They must pass this course to keep their assistantships. GTAs must also audit one of several model CO150 courses taught by regular faculty members.

Second-semester training. Again GTAs must enroll in E684 and teach a section of CO101 as well as a section of CO150. Their second semester of E684 replaces class meetings with in-service activities. Their two E684 instructors make at least three visits to each GTA's CO150 class during the semester and to provide counseling about the GTA's teaching. (The CO101 supervisor also continues to work with GTAs in CO101.) GTAs submit to their E684 instructors two sets of student papers for review of grading, write three progress reports, visit each other's classes, videotape class sessions, attend bimonthly group meetings, and solicit student evaluations at the end of the term. A "satisfactory" grade in E684 is necessary for renewal of the assistantship for a second year.

Second-year training. GTAs enroll in E684 each semester and continue to teach CO101 and CO150. Activities in E684 are minimal, consisting of review of student evaluations, visits or conferences if requested, and review of any significant changes in course syllabi or texts.

Course Descriptions

The following courses must be taken and/or taught by GTAs in the PIE program:

E684, Supervised College Teaching (3 semester credits, S/U grading). GTAs enroll in the course each semester that they teach for the department. During their first semester the course structure is traditional—three hours of class meetings a week. The only unusual feature is the in-service component centered on their CO101 teaching duties; evaluations by CO101 supervisors affect their overall class grades in E684. The E684 class has a lecture-discussion format, and it is devoted to review of, and testing on, the basics of good writing; study of the "standard" texts and syllabus used in CO150; work with various teaching techniques, assignments, exercises, group projects; practice in marking and grading; and exchange of ideas with peers. Subsequent semesters of E684 replace class activities with in-service requirements. Texts used are John C. Hodges and Mary Whitten's *Harbrace College Handbook* (8th ed., New York: Harcourt, 1977) and Jean Wyrick's *Steps to Writing Well* (New York: Holt, 1979).

CO101, Composition Fundamentals (2 credits, S/U grading). GTAs begin teaching this course concurrently with enrollment in E684. CO101 is a course for basic writers; it focuses on the writing of expository paragraphs, with work in grammar, diction, and spelling. Students do extensive in-class writing; GTA responsibilities are limited to two class hours and three conference/grading hours per week. All course materials and daily lesson plans are prepared by faculty CO101 supervisors, who also help GTAs with difficult papers and students. Class size is limited to twelve to fifteen persons, and most GTA time is spent giving individual attention to these students. Texts for the course are Robert B. Donald's *Writing Clear Paragraphs* (Englewood Cliffs, N.J.: Prentice-Hall, 1978) and Teresa F. Glazier's *The Least You Should Know about English* (New York: Holt, 1977).

CO150, College Writing (3 credits, traditional grading). GTAs teach this all-university requirement in their second and subsequent semesters. CO150 is a skills-oriented course that teaches students to write expository and argumentative prose. The course emphasizes logical development and support of ideas, effective organization, accepted conventions of mechanics and usage, and attention to appropriate style. It requires the drafting and revision of at least three extended paragraphs and five essays; quizzes; a midterm on grammar; and a final essay examination. First-year GTAs must teach from a standard syllabus and texts; second-year GTAs may develop their own material subject to faculty approval. The class is expected to demand fifteen hours per week of the GTA's twenty-hour contracted workload; while closely supervised, GTAs are responsible for all phases of CO150 instruction. Texts for the standard CO150 course are the *Harbrace College Handbook* and Wyrick's *Steps to Writing Well*.

Staffing and Funding

Staffing requirements. The PIE program trains twenty-eight GTAs in two-year cycles, or approximately fourteen "new" and fourteen "old" GTAs each year. Faculty assignments necessary for training and supervision are roughly equivalent to one FTE position (nine-hour load). The teaching of E684 requires one three-credit course assignment in fall semester and two in spring; CO101 supervision requires the equivalent of two three-credit course assignments in fall and one in spring. Perhaps one-fifth of the administrative time of the Director of Composition and his assistant is also required to coordinate the PIE effort with other elements of the overall composition program. (The director is given a one-course release each semester; his assistant a one-course release in summer or fall). The PIE program also requires that six or seven faculty members teach a model CO150 class in fall semester for GTA auditors; however, this time is "free" to the training program, since all our faculty regularly teach composition.

GTA employment status. GTAs hold nine-month appointments (20 August to 20 May), provided they pass E684 each semester; a contract signed before their first semester is normally renewed for a second year. First-year GTAs are paid $3,490 plus $859 (resident) or $3,066 (nonresident) tuition waiver per academic year; second-year GTAs receive $3,685 and waiver. Salaries are fixed at the college level and incorporated into the department's yearly budget allocation. GTAs are required to devote twenty hours per week to assistantship duties.

GTAs participate in department meetings and elect a voting representative to the Composition Committee; they also have a graduate organization to represent their interests. GTAs in danger of failing E684 (and thereby losing their jobs) are put on formal probation no later than the tenth week of each semester; a concentrated effort is then made by the faculty to help them correct deficiencies before the end of the term. If numerous or serious deficiencies are still in evidence at that time (e.g., poor teaching, grading, and performance on tests in E684), an "unsatisfactory" is given in E684 and the assistantship is terminated. If deficiencies are limited and the GTA shows significant improvement, probation is extended into the next semester. No GTA may stay on probation for more than two semesters. Terminated GTAs may appeal their grade in E684 using standard department and university student appeals procedures.

Prospects

While the new training program is still too new for all problems to surface, a few have already made themselves apparent. The most pressing occur in the Composition Fundamentals course. Simply put, GTAs need more time to learn how to cope with basic writers, and basic writers need more of the GTAs' time. A second source of distress has been a certain amount of GTA resistance to the rigor of the program; some feel that their appointments should not be so conditional and their performances not so patterned. The confrontation of freedom and authority is perhaps inevitable, but it causes problems and raises questions. And a final problem—at least potentially—is the program's cost. First-semester GTAs do very little teaching; a faculty position is devoted to GTA training. The benefits of this investment may not be obvious enough or statistically demonstrable enough to counter inevitable administrative demands for increased credit-hour production.

Although we plan to address these problems, too much stargazing at this point would be premature; we have scarcely begun to realize what we have. We will try to strengthen the CO101 component of the program; we will attempt to give GTAs the freedom and responsibility they deserve, perhaps involving them in university-wide cross-curricular activities; we will attempt to secure quantitative measurements of the program's effectiveness. We would of course like to expand our library, involve more faculty in training efforts, and add to our staff. Our prospects are good; we have the support of our department and a growing concern about student writing throughout the university. We will, of course, be fighting the same battles all higher education must fight; but we feel that the strengths of the training program just described will enable us to defend ourselves effectively.

Cornell University, Department of Modern Languages and Linguistics

James S. Noblitt

Background of the Summer Training Program

The summer training of teaching assistants in modern foreign languages at Cornell centers mainly on French, German, Russian, Spanish, and English as a foreign language. Although many other languages are taught, the need for a carefully developed program of apprenticeship is greatest in these languages, for a number of reasons. First, the number of undergraduates enrolled in the commonly taught languages requires many sections and a large teaching staff, too large for informal contacts with the course head to ensure adequate day-to-day training and guidance. Unlike our native-speaker lecturers, who often continue in service for a number of years, teaching assistants typically serve in a particular course for only about two years, and must achieve a rapid professional orientation if quality language instruction is to be maintained. This condition is especially true at Cornell, where the students have frequent contact with their TA in sections in which enrollment is limited to about ten students. The worth of a particular language course is viewed in student course evaluations as directly dependent on the pedagogical skill of the teaching assistant. Finally, for the languages mentioned, instruction at the elementary and intermediate levels is provided generally through the Department of Modern Languages and Linguistics; certain intermediate and all literature courses are offered through the departments of Romance Studies, German Literature, and Russian Literature. Thus language instruction in all of its aspects must be viewed as a joint program with close coordination and cooperation among departments. A given graduate student may teach for more than one department during his or her period of residence. Although each department has autonomy over its own courses, the selection of teaching assistants for language courses is made from the pool of available graduate students with the appropriate linguistic background.

The responsibility for organizing training in language pedagogy rests, for the languages mentioned, with the Department of Modern Languages and Linguistics, which has staff members with professional interests—including research and publications—in applied linguistics. In addition to receiving guidance from the course head for a specific teaching assignment, a teaching assistant may also take, for credit, a traditional course in the applied linguistics of a particular language. The most unusual feature of the apprenticeship, however, is the Cornell Summer Training Program, details of which are summarized below.

Objectives of the Summer Training Program

The Cornell Summer Training Program was conceived with a rather simple rationale: a professional language teacher needs, in addition to advanced foreign language skills, a practical knowledge of the particular methodology that he or she will use, a thorough understanding of the educational and linguistic bases for the methodology, and time in which to develop this new understanding and skill. The underlying assumptions are that effective language teaching may be achieved by providing linguistically qualified students an opportunity to understand thoroughly what they are trying to accomplish before they set foot in the classroom and that a sense of professionalism is, in itself, a highly motivating factor for the novice to excel in language instruction. We do not promise a single methodological approach that will finally solve all problems encountered in language instruction. On the contrary, we examine a number of methodologies that have proved effective in a given educational context, exploring their theoretical and practical bases from the complementary views of linguistics, psychology, and education. This approach is justified by what we perceive as a dual need on the part of an apprentice: the mastery of effective language teaching skills appropriate for an immediate course assignment at Cornell coupled with an understanding of how to select materials and a methodology appropriate to the educational context that may be encountered when the apprentice has an appointment at another institution.

Although limited, these goals are ambitious, especially if one cannot provide enough time to reflect thoughtfully on the issues raised and to master the fundamentals of the methodology employed. It is not controversial to observe that very little can be achieved in this respect by asking the novice teaching assistant to appear a day or two before classes in order to go over the syllabus and get acquainted with the textbook. This procedure implies that the major learning event for the graduate assistant will be on-the-job training and that the institution is prepared to accept the consequences of trial-and-error learning as the novice discovers what works and what does not. Although this effect cannot be totally dispelled by a six-week training course before teaching, the potentially excellent instructor can be spared the demoralizing effects of committing elementary errors in pedagogy because of simple ignorance of more effective techniques. The summer training period also allows time for the staff to assess the strengths and weaknesses of the trainees, which in turn permits optimal placement of an assistant at the appropriate course level and assists in determining whether further instruction in language skills is required. Training before the beginning of the school year helps us meet a primary objective, which is to avoid a situation in which graduate assistants are forced to choose between their own educational needs in pursuing a degree program and the needs of their students for competent classroom instruction. We cannot accept the proposition that a teaching assistantship is no more than a means for providing funds for graduate study. At its worst, unprofessional teaching demoralizes both student and teacher, embarrasses both the institution and the profession. If enough time is provided for a competent apprenticeship, that is, enough time to understand both what to do and how to do it before being called on to perform, the tension between the novices' learning and teaching can be minimized and their complementary roles more fully appreciated. Most important, we can more fully exploit the enormous goodwill that exists toward excellence in teaching.

Organization of the Program

Moving from a conviction that one's objectives are desirable, even feasible, to a funded program is not easy and may require some precipitating event in order to come to pass. In our case, the impetus was provided by an outside review of Cornell's foreign language program. One finding (which is apparently typical of many institutions) was that we were not fully exploiting the expertise available locally in preparing graduate students for teaching duties. Enormous resources in the areas of language study, psychology, and education were simply not being used or even brought to the attention of prospective teachers. Professor of Psychology (and then Dean of Arts and Sciences) Harry Levin asked me, as Professor of Applied Linguistics, to prepare an outline of a training program and estimated budget, promising university funds to initiate the enterprise. We estimated that we could accommodate about fifteen to twenty graduate students on a budget of approximately $25,000, and this estimate turned out to be accurate. Using the Cornell Summer Writing Workshop (established to train instructors for our freshman seminars) as a model, we decided to take advantage of the presence of students enrolled in foreign language classes during the summer in order to have a realistic setting for observation and occasional practice teaching. Practice teaching with peers or other volunteer students has the drawback of producing an artificial situation that lacks the important element of demonstrating the developmental aspects of second language acquisition. The possible detrimental effects of intruding in the classroom are offset by the benefits of making graduate students available as tutors for individual students. The trainees, in effect, function as teaching aides for the instructor in charge.

In order for the participating graduate apprentices to afford to attend the summer program, Levin suggested that a stipend be paid each participant. At $750 each, approximately one-half of the budget is allocated for stipends. Although minimal, this payment had made participation economically feasible for our trainees. Each participant in the noncredit program receives a letter for his or her file indicating completion of the program, which has proved extremely useful in securing positions in institutions where both teaching and scholarship are stressed. Every year since the program began the number of applicants has exceeded the number of openings; several asked to attend even without stipend. Students have applied from Linguistics, Romance Studies, German Literature, Russian Literature, and Comparative Literature. A few special students have been admitted from Asian Studies to observe our classes in Chinese and Japanese. The remaining half of the budget has been allocated to honoraria for special seminar leaders, salaries for a director and language supervisors for each of the language specialties, and for general expenses. Salaries are comparable to those paid for a two-credit summer-session course. It should be noted that it is difficult to retain qualified personnel during the summer months on a purely volunteer basis.

After the initial experiment in 1976, we were gratified at the warmth of the response from the participants. The most often repeated comment in the evaluations cited "increased confidence" as the major benefit. The reaction of the trainees confirmed what I had observed when I worked with the Danforth Foundation in training graduate assistants in various academic fields: novice teachers are most grateful for pedagogical preparation before they assume their duties, and they do not resent the time spent in the undertaking. (Indeed, they are dismayed when no provision is made.) Thus, when Alain Seznec, Professor of Romance Studies, assumed the office of Dean of Arts and Sciences, he promised continued support of the program, even though he was being asked at the same time to make serious cuts in the college's budget. He found funding through a grant from the Exxon Foundation, which has been interested in supporting innovations directed toward the improvement of undergraduate education.

Operation of the Program

Morning sessions (one to two hours) of the program are under the direction of the individual language supervisors. Trainees observe about three times a week and teach at least two fifty-minute sessions under close supervision during the summer. A detailed critique and a discussion follow each practice session. In addition, the trainees attend a practicum twice a week, which is devoted to contrastive analysis, a detailed examination of the textbook materials in use, training in methodology, and practical advice on dialogue presentation and grammar explanation. Afternoon sessions (1½ hours) are conducted by the director and invited lecturers. The trainees begin with three afternoons of a spoken-language workshop in learning an unfamiliar language. (Cantonese, Rumanian, and Japanese have been used so far.) The workshop demonstrates practical techniques for the first meetings of a spoken-language course and makes the participants sensitive to the experience their own students will be undergoing in class. Next begin lectures and topics for discussion, which progress somewhat in parallel. On the one hand there are presentations, by invited members of the various literature departments, of techniques for eliciting discussions of readings in various genres and for approaching problems in writing a foreign language at different levels. These seminars, held twice weekly, are designed to dispel any artificial separation between the teaching of language and literature. They provide an interesting forum for graduate students in literature and linguistics to share ideas on the methodology of teaching reading. On the other hand there are, three times a week, lectures on topics of professional interest in applied linguistics. These are designed to give a rapid orientation to the state of the art of foreign language teaching. Topics include the influence of findings in psycholinguistics on language-acquisition theory, the history of language teaching in the United States, factors influencing the design of textbooks, the role of aptitude and motivation in foreign language study, and testing design. In addition we discuss the concerns of the educational establishment for requirements, grading, student counseling, classroom management, and syllabus design. We attempt to assess the feasibility of teaching for bilingualism at the college level and explore the cultural benefits of foreign language study. Six weeks appear to be minimally adequate for accomplishing our program objectives.

Graduate students respond very positively to the program, particularly in gaining a sense of professionalism in foreign language teaching. The heart of the matter lies in communicating an academic interest in observing the unfolding of language skills in one's own students. Once this is seen, in all its complexity, the teaching of an elementary course can become both a challenging and a rewarding experience. We try to show how effective teaching requires a perfect understanding of one's educational objectives, a mastery of techniques for achieving these objectives, and a highly developed sense of empathy for the student's point of view. The challenge to the teacher lies in orchestrating a large number of variables in order to optimize the learning experience for every individual in the classroom. Although only some of our trainees become outstanding teachers, all are aware of the elements of excellence in foreign language teaching.

Apprenticeship in the Program

The following points summarize the general provisions for an apprenticeship. We admit about fifteen of the twenty-five or so summer applicants each year, distributed as equally as possible among the language specialties. Top priority for acceptance is given applicants who will teach the following semester and who have had no previous training or teaching experience. (Ideally, first-year graduate students are not appointed as TAs in order to allow time for an orientation to graduate study and improvement of language skills, if necessary, before teaching.) Other students are admitted as funds allow, since it is to everyone's advantage for future professionals to have had the training provided, even if they will not be teaching at this university.

After the summer training program, a student may take for credit a course in the applied linguistics of his or her language specialty. There are, in addition, weekly meetings with the course head for further (noncredit) training and guidance. Minors in applied linguistics are required to take the course in Second Language Acquisition (or the equivalent) during the spring semester.

Graduate teaching assistants are typically assigned a course at the elementary or intermediate level, which meets three or four times a week. (Difficult languages, like Russian, meet five times a week.) A particularly well-qualified student occasionally teaches an advanced course. To illustrate, elementary courses in French, German, and Spanish meet four times a week in recitation with a teaching assistant; the courses meet once a week for a lecture by the professor who is course head. Graduate assistants are also responsible for at least one hour per week of office consultation with their students. The course head makes periodic visits to classes and discusses his or her evaluation with each teaching assistant visited. These evaluations provide the basis for subsequent appointments and for letters of recommendation.

Graduate assistants receive a stipend of about $4,000, plus tuition, fees, and medical benefits. They are appointed on a yearly basis according to the recommendation of the course head. It is difficult to secure an assistantship after the fourth year of teaching, since there is increasing pressure to distribute assistantships among those eligible for graduate support. There is no union for graduate assistants; grievances are handled at the lowest possible point in the hierarchy of course head, departmental chairman, dean, and provost. Formal petitions may be submitted to the appropriate field representative for faculty action. The safeguards provided by the University Judicial Code are naturally available to all students.

Prospects and Difficulties

The immediate benefits of the program are reflected in the teaching assistants' sense of satisfaction with success in the classroom. We have found, in reviewing the undergraduate course evaluations, high praise for the professional aspects of their TAs' teaching (organization, preparation, enthusiasm) and far fewer complaints about poorly qualified graduate assistants. Another benefit, a bit more subtle to assess, lies in the interest that recently appointed assistant professors show in what their assistants are doing; they ask to see reading lists and often sit in on lectures and demonstrations in order to pick up information on topics of professional interest. Their interest provides, indirectly, new faculty training. A third and perhaps most significant benefit, thoroughly in keeping with the spirit of the Exxon grant, is that other departments that are considering a training program can examine our model. Last year the Chemistry Department began summer training of TAs; it is likely that other departments, sensitive to complaints of high tuition and poor instruction, will follow suit if they can find interested personnel and funding.

The major problem, in my view, is not convincing others of the worth of such a program but promoting the priority of teacher training to the point that it is regularly provided for and funded in the same way that other operations in institutions of higher learning are. Unless deans fight for the funding, teacher training programs will expire as soon as the energy and goodwill of interested individuals are exhausted. Good teacher training begins at the departmental level, where the problems are well understood; but grass roots initiatives must be matched with support from the top.

East Carolina University, Department of English

Bertie E. Fearing and Erwin Hester

Founded as a teachers college in 1907, East Carolina University has retained its commitment to the training of teachers while it has expanded to a multipurpose university. The English Department, like other academic departments, offers a degree program that leads to secondary certification as well as traditional liberal arts degrees; as part of the certification program, appropriately qualified faculty in the English Department teach "methods" courses, supervise student teachers, and assume many other responsibilities associated with training secondary school English teachers. Thus, the English Department's decision to develop a graduate level program for the preparation of two-year college English teachers seemed to be a natural extension of the program for training secondary teachers already offered by the department; further, the experience with teacher training at the secondary level provided the department with readily available models for a two-year college teacher training program. The patterns were at hand; the content for the program came from experienced practitioners of two-year college English teaching.

Development

A person with several years' experience as a successful two-year college English teacher was added to our faculty in 1973 and charged with the principal responsibility of developing a program for two-year college English teachers. The "Guidelines for Junior College English Teacher Training Programs," which had been recently published by the National Council of Teachers of English (in *College Composition and Communication*, 22 [1971], was, of course, a primary resource for the committee that designed the Graduate Program for

Two-Year College English Teachers. The English Department also enlisted the aid of specialists in two-year college English from the North Carolina Department of Community Colleges and of several leading English teachers in North Carolina community colleges and technical institutes. The program that is described here was designed to meet the NCTE "Guidelines" and was shaped in large part by experienced and professionally active two-year college English teachers.

Administration

Although East Carolina's Program for Two-Year College English Teachers is a post-M.A. option, it is administered along with the regular M.A. program. Students in the Two-Year College Program are advised by the Director of Graduate Studies in English, who is responsible for advising all M.A. candidates. Students in the program first complete a strong traditional M.A., which requires a thesis and a comprehensive examination covering the conventional areas of British and American literature. Since most of the thirty to thirty-five full-time M.A. candidates in our program are also working as teaching assistants with full responsibility for teaching one and sometimes two sections of freshman composition each semester, they usually take two academic years to complete the M.A.; completion of the Two-Year College option may take at least part of an additional year.

Admission

Since the Graduate Program for Two-Year College English Teachers augments the M.A. in English, M.A. candidates are eligible to enter the program at any time, although they usually wait until their second year to do so. In-service teachers who already hold an M.A. and who teach in a two-year college are admitted to the program on an ad hoc basis.

Teaching Preparation Courses

The first prerequisite for teaching in a two-year college is a strong academic background in English studies. Of the thirty semester hours required for the M.A. in English, prospective teachers take at least three hours in linguistics—Modern Grammar, Linguistics and Cultural History of the English Language, or Descriptive Linguistics—and three hours in a nontraditional kind of literature—Special Studies in Film, Teaching Film in English Studies, or The Folk Literature of the English-Speaking World. Following the academic courses and before the teaching internship, program participants undertake two teaching preparation courses—Methods of Teaching English in the Two-Year College and Problems in Teaching College Composition—and they are urged to take a third, Developmental English in the Two-Year College. These teaching preparation courses and the internship add from ten to thirteen semester hours to the thirty-hour requirement for the M.A.

Methods of Teaching English in the Two-Year College, a three-hour course offered each fall semester, acquaints prospective teachers with the history, philosophy, and goals of the open admissions two-year college; with the variety and types of students and courses in the two-year college; and with traditional and innovative teaching methods. There are no texts; rather, students read widely in standard works about the community/junior college, in sociological studies about the nontraditional student, and in professional and pedagogical journals about the two-year college English curriculum. Individual course units focus on the vocational, technical, and college-parallel segments of the community college English program and on the various courses taught within these segments—everything from remedial reading to career communication skills to college-parallel literature courses. Outstanding English instructors from community colleges are invited as guest lecturers to address the graduate class on a regular basis. In addition, each class member makes a field visit to a different two-year college English department and attends at least one conference of a professional organization. Meetings such as the South Atlantic Modern Language Association, the Southeastern Conference on English in the Two-Year College, the North Carolina–Virginia College English Association, and the North Carolina Community College Conference give students a realistic look into the nature of college teaching.

Offered along with the methods course is an in-depth course on Problems in Teaching College Composition. This three-hour course familiarizes future instructors with the scope of writing courses taught in two-year colleges, namely freshman composition, business and technical writing, and creative writing. A blend of theory and application, the course probes the suitability and effectiveness of textbooks, approaches, and methods by exploring the canons and the most current literature on rhetorical and applied rhetorical theory. Writing as a process is stressed in the unit on freshman composition; communications theory, clarity, and objectivity in the unit on business and technical writing; and genre, imagery, and point of view in the unit on creative writing. Not only do participants study about writing, they also teach one another how to write, and, most important, they write—everything from a freshman essay to a technical report to a creative bit of prose.

The third teaching preparation course, Developmental English in the Two-Year College, is strongly recommended as an elective in the spring semester. Offering three hours credit, this course investigates linguistic research and examines the practical application of that research to diagnosis and remediation of deficiencies in reading and writing. The course also relies on standard works in the fields of linguistics and reading and on current periodical literature.

These three courses are taught by professors of English, two of whom are veteran community college teachers and one of whom is a regular workshop consultant for community colleges. A second strength of the program is its sponsorship of *Teaching English in the Two-Year College*, the only national journal published exclusively for two-year college English teachers. The journal is an open forum through which two-year college English teachers address issues and share ideas. Refereed articles offer practical suggestions for teaching reading, basic writing, composition, technical communications, literature, and the myriad courses taught in the two-year college. In addition, the journal runs a regular "News, Notes, and Announcements" feature to inform readers of current activities and events and publishes book reviews to alert readers to new textbooks. Thus, the journal gives our faculty and students a unique opportunity for staying abreast of the latest professional innovations and developments in the field. A third strength is provided by the School of Education, which offers such specialized courses as The Adult Learner, Design of Multimedia Instructional Materials, and Foundations and Curriculum Development.

The Teaching Internship

The Teaching Internship, a four-hour credit course offered in the spring semester, is the culminating experience for participants in the program. In-service teachers serve their internships in their home institutions under the cognizance of their department heads in collaboration with the university supervisor. Prospective teachers serve their internships in one of several nearby community colleges, where for one quarter they become teaching, albeit unpaid, colleagues. "New" interns are guided by experienced, successful community college "lead instructors" and by the university supervisor. The aim of the internship is to provide interns practical, wide-range experience in teaching several different courses and in assuming various related professional responsibilities, such as selecting textbooks, attending committee meetings, and designing courses.

Although no internship is exactly like another because of the many varied facets of community college English programs, interns typically assume full responsibility for teaching a nontransfer vocational or technical English course for one quarter, observe and teach three other courses for two weeks each, and work on an individual basis with developmental students in a lab setting for two weeks. Courses that may be assigned include developmental reading, basic writing, freshman composition, business correspondence, technical writing, oral communications, and various survey and specialized literature courses.

Along with their teaching assignments, interns spend a minimum of twelve hours a week on the community college campus, keeping office hours, attending departmental and committee meetings, conferring with lead teachers, and generally absorbing the campus atmosphere and adjusting to the somewhat frantic pace (an eighteen-hour course load is not unusual in community colleges in North Carolina). In addition, interns keep a log of their professional activities, attend a series of seminars on the university campus, and write a summary evaluation of their internship.

The supervision and evaluation of an intern are conducted by the community college lead teacher and the university supervisor. The lead teacher, who must have a M.A. in English and at least three years' teaching experience, designs the program for the intern, orients the intern to the school, and provides ongoing counseling and guidance through informal daily contact. The lead teacher also ensures that all instructional services (e.g., typing, duplicating, audiovisual equipment) are available to the intern. Usually, the class for which the intern has full-quarter responsibility comes from the course load of the lead teacher. Thus, a one-course reduced load is the only compensation for lead teachers—that and the knowledge that they have initiated a new colleague in the right way.

The university supervisor, an Assistant Professor of English and Coordinator of the Program, has the initial responsibility of arranging the internship with a two-year college, although the intern makes the appointment with the department head and interviews for the internship position. During the internship, the supervisor makes several visits to the community college to ensure that the internship is beneficial for all involved. Since the teaching internship counts as a course for the supervisor, there is no other compensation. Together the supervisor and the lead teacher, with the aid of student evaluations of the intern and the intern's own self-evaluation, determine the grade for the intern. Both the lead teacher and the supervisor write letters of recommendation, which go into the intern's dossier.

There has been no need to establish grievance procedures, for both the lead teachers and the interns have pronounced the Teaching Internship a resounding success. The lead teachers have found the interns exceptionally well-prepared for their teaching responsibilities, and the interns have found the internship an invaluable transition from the cloistered halls of academe to the raw realities of teaching in an open-admissions classroom.

Problems and Prospects

The long-standing commitment to excellence in teacher training by the English Department at East Carolina has secured for the Two-Year College Program a degree of faculty support that such a program might not have received in a department without a similar tradition of diversity. It seems, however, that some tension inevitably arises when a program of professional training is yoked to an M.A. program that retains the traditional emphasis on British and American literature. Some graduates of the Two-Year College Program have urged an increase in the proportion of the courses that deal with specific pedagogical problems encountered in the two-year college; others are grateful for the security of the traditional M.A. in English. This divergence of opinion is not likely to soon go away. A focal point for discussion, especially among the faculty, is the M.A. thesis: should a pedagogically oriented project be permitted or should the department hold a hard line, allowing only traditional topics in literary history or criticism? Topics in linguistics and rhetoric have provided a compromise between the practical and the traditional, but a final policy has been difficult to formulate.

Viewed from a more objective perspective, however, the varying attitudes in the department probably create a healthy tension, or balance, between the academic and the pedagogical. For when students in the Two-Year College Program complete the thirty hours of academic study, the specialized teaching preparation courses, and the internship, they are not only well schooled in traditional British and American literature, they are also well acquainted with the multifaceted aspects of teaching English in the two-year college and well prepared to begin their careers as classroom teachers: they are knowledgeable of literary scholarship and criticism, thoroughly versed in professional and pedagogical literature, and keenly aware of their own obligation and responsibility to contribute new knowledge to the field as practicing teacher-scholars.

East Texas State University, Department of Literature and Languages

Jon Jonz and Richard Fulkerson

About ten years ago the Department of Literature and Languages at East Texas State University saw an opportunity to strengthen its doctoral program by creating a teaching internship component. The course work for the previous, more traditional degree was not radically revised; rather, a series of pedagogically oriented courses and experiences were added to produce a hybrid program that emphasizes the college teaching of English.

History

With the encouragement and guidance of the Texas State Coordinating Board of Colleges and Universities, East Texas State University in 1969 began phasing out its Ph.D. in Literature (or Linguistics) in favor of a new Ed.D. in the College Teaching of English. Though the change from a Ph.D. to an Ed.D. may have been a mistake, the Department of Literature and Languages now has a well-established program that prepares postsecondary teachers for full participation in the profession. We are able to make this broad claim because we did not reject our traditional doctoral emphases in favor of a pedagogical emphasis. Instead, we added a sequence of pedagogical components to the existing Ph.D. requirements. The result is a demanding but effective degree program, requiring our students to be both teachers and scholars.

Though such a change, at a time when new doctoral programs were appearing practically overnight, might seem to have invited a sharp decline in enrollment, our experience has confirmed the basic wisdom of the change. Even though our Ed.D. is long and rigorous, it has grown steadily, attracting committed and energetic students. In the fall of 1969 the department produced only thirty-six doctoral credit hours, and it was not until the spring of 1973 that the first Ed.D. was awarded. Since that time, however, credit-hour production has steadily risen to a peak of 244 semester credit hours for the fall of 1978. After seven students were graduated in the spring of 1979, our fall 1979 production dropped off slightly to 216, but current applications portend another period of growth. At a time when other departments bemoan dwindling graduate enrollment, the Department of Literature and Languages with its hybrid degree looks toward a bright future.

Organization of the Program

The program involves most of the department's faculty in teaching internship-related courses, but five key faculty positions provide the overall control and direction to the program. These positions rotate at approximately three-year intervals so as to provide fresh perspectives and to distribute responsibility among a large number of faculty members. The program is ultimately staffed, then, by nearly all of the department.

The five positions that contribute most visibly to the continuity of the program are the Head of the Department, the Chairman of the Committee on Screening and Appointments, the Coordinator of Interns, the Coordinator of Composition, and the Director of the Communication Skills Center. These positions are mutually exclusive, and each position holder has a primary responsibility outside the doctoral program. None is compensated specifically for participation in the program, and each position has changed hands at least once since the program's inception—most two or more times.

Other than the various faculty members who teach the required core of courses and those who lead the internship colloquiums, the major guidance for the program comes from the Committee on Screening and Appointments. Besides its principal function of recruiting and selecting qualified candidates for graduate degrees, the committee also oversees the courses and the concentrations in the program. The committee coordinates the program by funneling recommendations from the various doctoral concentration-area committees to the entire graduate faculty for action. In addition to the chairman of the committee and two at-large graduate faculty members, the committee consists of the key administrators cited earlier.

Screening

The selection and appointment procedure that recommends new interns is rigorous. After meeting standard university requirements, candidates for positions in the doctoral internship program must demonstrate high verbal ability on the Graduate Record Examination, must have a distinguished undergraduate and postgraduate record, and must present strong personal and professional recommendations. Additionally, each prospective student undergoes a thorough screening interview, either in person or by telephone. During this interview the members of the Committee on Screening and Appointments examine the prospective student's experience, education, attitudes, and career objectives from their unique points of view. The Coordinator of Composition, for example, may ask about the prospective intern's orientation toward teaching (and learning) writing, while the Director of the Communication Skills Center may concentrate on individual instruction. At the same time, the interviewee can question the members of the committee regarding *their* viewpoints, attitudes toward the program, and knowledge of program operation. The interview, then, is as much an opportunity for the prospective program participant to learn about the requirements of the degree as it is an opportunity for faculty members to gather information and impressions needed to make decisions about admitting or rejecting the candidate. For the prospective intern, the interview helps clarify the objectives and components of the program, and for the committee it allows the personal screening for which no amount of paper documentation can substitute.

Program Description

The graduate internship program in English at East Texas has the central goal of preparing young teacher-scholars to assume positions of professional responsibility at the postsecondary level. At every juncture in their university experience, our interns find themselves involved in challenging discussions and exploration of theory as well as in the practical, day-to-day problem solving related to their teaching and tutoring assignments. Students seeking the master's degree in English may choose from concentrations in composition, literature, or linguistics, or they may opt for a comprehensive program that embraces all three. At the doctoral level, students may choose one of five areas of concentration. At either level or in any concentration, however, interns are involved in a carefully planned, coordinated sequence of experiences that relate their academic pursuits and interests to the pragmatic demands of teaching college English. The internship program is optional at the master's level, and many of our master's students are public school teachers who have no plans to teach at the postsecondary level. At the doctoral level, however, all our students, even those doing creative dissertations, must be in the internship program and must convince us that their career objectives, however specific, focus on the teaching of college English. Though this essay describes the doctoral internship program, it should be understood that some of our students begin their internships directly out of undergraduate school and that some go no further than the master's degree.

The doctoral program requires at least ninety semester hours of study beyond the baccalaureate, of which at least seventy hours must be in English and cognate subjects. Of these seventy hours in the major field, at least twenty-seven must be in an area of concentration and at least thirty-six must be distributed in four cognate minors and in the broad field of the humanities. In addition, there is a two-year, research-tool foreign language requirement, and the student must pass a sixteen-hour written qualifying examination on the specialization and minors before starting the dissertation.

Every student chooses a major area of concentration (at least twenty-seven hours, including the dissertation), and to facilitate that choice the department tries to be as flexible as resources and logistics allow. Students may therefore specialize in American literature, British literature, linguistics, comparative literature, a literary genre, or most recently, composition and rhetoric. Students may then write dissertations on traditional literary subjects, on linguistic topics, stylistics, and so on, or they may do an original literary work (for genre specialists). Recently completed dissertations include such diverse topics as Arabic influences on Chaucer, folklore in southwestern American fiction, Charles Dickens and the self-denying woman, and dialect surveys of various regions in Texas. Currently, students are working on Twain, black drama, and musical structure in Tennessee Williams. We do not allow purely pedagogical research for the dissertation, partly because we feel that it is still the province of the College of Education and partly because each student does a major pedagogical research project as part of required course work.

Scholarship and Internship

In order to achieve our goal of preparing graduates to become effective faculty members, all doctoral students participate in both scholarly study and in pedagogical preparation from the beginning of their doctoral work. The scholarly study consists of extensive course work in both the student's specialization and the related minor fields, including a required course in literary research techniques as well as the written qualifying examination and the dissertation. To this extent our program is similar to many American doctoral programs in literature, linguistics, and/or composition.

In addition to this standard core program, however, our doctorate is unusual in that it requires a pedagogical internship, a complex of several elements designed to ensure that graduates will be prepared not only as scholars but also as teachers, ready to assume faculty positions in higher education. The internship requires that, for at least one year, the graduate student hold the position of assistant instructor in the department. On the doctoral level, interns may not hold appointments for more than three years, but interns who start at the master's level may hold appointments for an additional two years, making a total of five years of supported study possible. Most interns hold appointments for several years. As an assistant instructor (or intern), the graduate student has a carefully guided experience in being an apprentice member of an English department. The internship involves three interrelated features designed to prepare the student as an effective teacher: (1) pedagogical courses, (2) professional colloquiums, and (3) supervised teaching and tutoring.

All interns take the following courses in English pedagogy:

The Teaching of English in College (English 571)
Independent Research in English Pedagogy (English 677)
two approved courses in the College of Education

In these courses, the intern is introduced to both practical classroom procedures and theoretical issues about English education as well as to the major pedagogical literature. All assistant instructors take English 571 during the first fall that they are in the program. Taught by the Coordinator of Interns, it is an extensive introduction to the methods, theories, problems, and techniques of teaching college English. In English 677, taught each spring, the intern will build on that background to prepare a major pedagogical research paper. These papers often result in presentations at the local, state, or national conferences, which our students are regularly encouraged to attend and participate in. As their approved education courses outside the department, most interns take a course in Educational Media and Technology; many elect one in the American Junior/Community College.

At the same time that interns take one of these pedagogical courses and two additional courses in literature, linguistics, or composition, they also participate in a professional colloquium—at least for the first two years that the appointment is held. The colloquiums are informal weekly meetings of a group of interns with one faculty member and are devoted to practical discussion of such matters as classroom management, grading, lesson plans, and university procedures and regulations. These colloquiums are three-hour courses graded on a pass/fail basis. Since our program is small (limited to about 22 interns at any one time), the colloquiums (like most graduate courses) usually have no more than ten students. The colloquium leader is responsible for the direct supervision of the intern's teaching and any other professional guidance warranted at that stage of the intern's preparation.

The first-year colloquiums are led by the Coordinator of Composition, who guides the interns carefully through the standard freshman composition sequence following a syllabus designed for the intern's guidance. The coordinator provides suggestions about classroom activities and tricks of the trade during the weekly meetings, observes each intern in the classroom at least once a semester, submits a written report to the intern about the observation, and guides the intern's grading and marking of student papers. During the second year, the weekly colloquiums continue, focusing on a variety of professional matters ranging from alternative classroom procedures to preparing a curriculum vitae and handling a job interview, and from the problems and approaches of remediation to submitting manuscripts for publication. In recent years, colloquiums have been directed by the Department Head, the Director of Interns, the ex-Coordinator of Composition, and the Director of the Communication Skills Center. Such rotation exposes the interns to a variety of pedagogical approaches. Whoever directs the second-year colloquiums is still responsible for observing each intern at work and for monitoring grading and marking practices.

The key element of the internship, toward which both the colloquiums and the pedagogical courses are directed, is the actual teaching done by each assistant instructor. The assistant instructor's teaching load is two courses or the equivalent. In practice, this leads to a variety of possible assignments. A first-year intern might teach two courses each semester in the normal freshman-composition sequence (with the guidance provided by the colloquiums and the pedagogical courses). Currently, the new intern is more likely to teach one course every semester and fulfill the remainder of the appointment by tutoring ten hours a week in either the Reading Center or the Writing Center (the two divisions of the Communication Skills Center). If tutoring is part of the assignment, the intern receives special training in workshops held during the first two weeks of the semester. Whatever the duties, we take pains to guide and monitor the intern's work, especially during the first year.

Although guided practical experience characterizes each year of the internship, in each succeeding year the intern becomes more independent and professionally responsible. In the second year, colloquiums continue, but the intern is responsible for selecting textbooks and designing syllabi within the departmental course guidelines, just as are full members of the department. Intern teaching assignments are also likely to broaden. Some interns become members of the department's developmental language skills staff and teach sections of developmental English. Some work into teaching English as a second language, some teach sophomore introductions to literature, and some teach developmental or speed reading courses under the guidance of the reading-course coordinator. In the third year of internship, colloquiums are no longer required, but the diverse and guided classroom preparation continues.

As assistant instructors, interns are full-fledged junior members of the department. They hold nine-month renewable appointments, with the possibility of summer work. They are elected to most departmental committees, and all are invited to participate in monthly departmental faculty meetings. They are the teachers of record in their classes, and they edit the departmental publications of student writing: *Write-On* for freshman essays and paragraphs and *Forthcoming* for creative works by advanced undergraduate and graduate students.

By the time they graduate, our interns have taught a variety of lower-division courses under close supervision, they have dealt with students on a one-to-one basis in the Skills Center, they have participated in discussions of pedagogical theory and practice, and they have read the major books on teaching English. They have become familiar with the major textbooks, approaches, journals, and organizations related to teaching English, they have participated in faculty and committee meetings, and they have attended conferences, usually having presented papers. They will even have been taught the finer points of preparing abstracts of their own papers. In short, they will have had the opportunity to become involved in most of the professional activities and to confront most of the issues they will meet once they accept that first full-time faculty appointment. Our graduates are already experienced professionals.

Some Current Problems

East Texas State University graduates are not plagued with the unemployment problems that often accompany the English doctorate. Their preparation has been designed to make them attractive candidates for faculty positions that emphasize teaching undergraduate courses, as well as for research-oriented positions on graduate faculties. To date, each of our Ed.D. graduates has received an offer from a postsecondary institution; nearly all currently teach college English full time. Our constant focus on that goal and our mixture of purely academic study with practical classroom experience is clearly successful.

We do have a variety of other problems, however. Chief among them is the limited number of graduate assistantships available to the department. Since our doctorate requires at least one year of supervised college-level teaching, the availability of assistantships absolutely constrains our program's size. Only rarely are we able to arrange an "externship" at other local or regional institutions, and even then we prefer that it be our faculty that supervises the experience. Currently we have been assigned about twenty-two assistantships, including those designated for the Communication Skills Center. Our future growth is clearly a function of the increase in that number.

A related problem involves the timing of local budgetary decisions. In recent years the department has lost a number of sufficiently qualified applicants because of its inability to notify applicants early enough that assistantships are available. Even though they would prefer to enter our program, applicants frequently discover that they must accept other offers simply because those offers are tendered before ours possibly can be.

A further problem is that we appear to offer a doctorate of education when in fact ours is a hybrid degree. We would probably fare better in some respects were the degree to be a Ph.D. in the College Teaching of English. We have occasional difficulties in recruiting since prospective interns generally prefer the Ph.D., but our placement record is usually sufficient to persuade applicants of the quality of our Ed.D. We have also seen problems when our graduates enter the job market. Announcements often specify the Ph.D. rather than the generic "doctorate," and some institutions will not consider hiring the Ed.D. holder, even though ours is not the College of Education degree. Furthermore, at some institutions Ed.D. holders are even paid on a lower salary scale than Ph.D. holders. The disparity is usually removed, however, once we explain what our program involves. Nevertheless, we are currently studying the advisability of changing the initials.

Other problems include the relatively low pay for assistant instructors (somewhat offset by the low cost of living in Commerce, Texas) and the feeling among the interns that taking three courses and a colloquium while teaching two courses or the equivalent demands too much time and energy.

The Future

Since we are pleased with both the placement record and the job performance of our graduates, there will be no major shifts in the direction of our internship program. We will continue with several developments already in progress, such as strengthening the graduate offerings in composition and expanding the Communication Skills Center. We are currently shifting English 699 (Research

Methods) from being a terminal course related to the dissertation to being an early course to aid the student in all graduate course work. Perhaps one or more of the education course requirements may be modified, and possibly the Ed.D. will once again be a Ph.D. All in all, however, the essential features of this apprenticeship program, developed successfully over the past decade, will continue without major modification.

Indiana University, Department of English

Michael C. Flanigan

Background of the Program

Teacher apprentices at Indiana University attend preservice and in-service workshops, team teach with a faculty member and three or four other teaching assistants, are visited by the Director of Composition and his staff, receive written training materials for each course they teach, have access to videotapes that are designed to help them with their teaching, may sign up for colloquiums on teaching, and may minor in the teaching of composition by taking appropriate course work. The present program for training teacher apprentices developed slowly as a result of changes in the 1960s. In the early 1960s all TAs teaching elementary composition were expected to follow a common day-by-day syllabus administered by the Director of First-Year Studies. The training TAs received consisted mostly of trying to figure out how to implement the prescribed plans using rhetorics, handbooks, and readers. Little discussion of basic issues in teaching composition took place in weekly meetings. At the same time, in the introductory literature courses L101 and L102 (great-book courses), other TAs served as readers and most of what they learned was how to grade papers and exams to the satisfaction of the faculty member in charge. They did no formal teaching.

The rigid elementary composition syllabus of the early sixties turned out to be unmanageable and unproductive, and it gave way to the cry for more freedom. By the late sixties the course was characterized by its shapelessness and anarchy and, as one former Director of First-Year Studies said, "It was a real mess." TAs received little help in teaching the course except for what they quickly picked up from other TAs. The introductory literature course (normally enrolling 250 students) began to lose students when the literature requirement was changed. During the same period the composition requirement was reduced from three courses to one.

To ensure that TAs received more help with teaching and to accommodate changes in enrollment the department, in the late sixties, created a new course called Introduction to Writing and the Study of Literature. The course enrolled 250 students in faculty-designed large lecture sections, which in turn were broken down into ten discussion sections run by TAs. The TAs were supervised and visited by faculty members: they learned how to lead discussions, design writing assignments, grade papers and tests, and do whatever else faculty members could help them with in their weekly meetings. As many new TAs as possible were assigned to this course before they were allowed to teach courses with no built-in supervision. Around the same time that this new course was established round-table discussions of teaching were introduced and many TAs took part in these. Also, the department created special internship courses on the teaching of literature and composition. These were conducted on an individual basis with a TA working directly with a faculty member by assisting in a course the faculty member was teaching.

While many innovations were made in training TAs during this period, the nature of the program was informal and many TAs received little help. Although much was being done for TAs in the writing-literature course, TAs in the elementary composition course were "pretty much ignored." In the early seventies the department changed its policy of appointing a new Director of First-Year Studies every two years to appoint a person who would continue in the position for as long as he wished. The new person was hired because he had a special interest in training apprentices, a good background in rhetoric and composition, and a commitment to research and publishing in both areas.

The new Director of First-Year Studies' first action was to begin writing course manuals for each course TAs taught. The goal was not to set up a single system but to create working documents that would serve as points of reference for instruction, discussion, and research. Next, preservice and in-service workshops were established. Then an elaborate system of supportive classroom observations was begun.[1] Because the elementary writing course needed the most attention, special workshops were run and a set of videotapes for individualized instruction was developed.[2] Also, cooperative efforts led to faculty members teaching the introductory writing-literature course and experiments with special courses for TAs; the director participated in sections of the writing-literature course, and special visitation programs were initiated among TAs and the staff of the First-Year Studies office. At the request of TAs in the department a minor in the Teaching of Composition was established. The minor allowed TAs to take course work in the theory and practice of rhetoric and composition, design and evaluate their own course, and experiment with their own writing as they read about various approaches to writing advocated by leaders in the profession.

Objectives and Organization

Initially the primary goal of all efforts to establish a teacher apprentice program was to improve instruction within the department. As the program evolved, however, special attention was given to helping individual teachers come to a better understanding of how they best functioned as individuals and teachers. The usual demand to perform with excellence immediately was diminished as much as possible, and serious work in "how to teach" and in exploring various methods was encouraged.[3] All funding for the program came from English Department resources, except for the two-year development of the videotapes designed to improve college teaching. As the visitation program from the First-Year Studies office was expanded two experienced TAs, with work in the minor in the Teaching of Composition, were assigned to the director. They also assisted in running workshops and working with special groups of TAs who taught special students or who were given teaching assignments after the formal workshops in the fall.

Ostensibly the program is under the control of the Director of First-Year

Studies (now known as the Director of Composition). He runs preservice and in-service workshops, directs the visitation program, oversees the design of courses taught by TAs, coordinates courses in the Teaching of Composition, chairs the work of the Composition Committee, sits on the TA Selection Committee, and administers the day-to-day concerns related to TAs. But faculty members teaching the introductory writing-literature course supervise the TAs who teach with them. The faculty member designs the course but often leaves room for TAs to make contributions. Most faculty members hold weekly meetings with their TAs to discuss the direction of the course, how to give assignments, how to grade, how to involve students in the process of writing, and how to deal with a host of other concerns related to teaching. The structure allows TAs to work as a team and to share and discuss ideas with others engaged in the same teaching problems they are facing. Often an experienced TA is assigned to a group of new TAs in the introductory writing-literature course. This design not only lets new TAs benefit from the experience of a mature colleague but gives recognition to the experienced TA.

Program Stages

TAs are selected for the program mainly from the group of graduate students in residence. Rarely is anyone with less than a year's work in the department selected, but three to six outside applicants with master's degrees are appointed each year. Also, any graduate student who receives a scholarship in the department or an appointment as a reader is usually appointed a TA when the scholarship or readership runs out. Appointments, which run for two to four years, are made by the Associate Instructors (TA) Selection Committee, whose members represent all ranks in the department.

The criteria for selection are laid out in a memo sent to prospective TAs by the chairperson on the committee. Part of her memo reads:

> We pay attention to the whole of your record: no single element decides the success or failure of your application. The following criteria, however —not listed in any order of priority—have been most frequently noted in past decisions:
> (1) extent of progress toward degree, including language exams and qualifying exams passed, hours of credit accumulated, etc.;
> (2) range and nature of course work completed;
> (3) letters of recommendation;
> (4) GPA;
> (5) number of Incompletes still on record, together with explanations for their presence;
> (6) indications of teaching potential (as might be demonstrated, for example, by tutoring experience, enrollment in pedagogical courses, or by comments of teachers);
> (7) other forms of experience related to teachers (jobs, for example, or volunteer work, or travel, or special study).

After the applicants have been ranked by the committee the top twenty or so are appointed TAs and a few others of lower ranking are made readers. As resignations occur in the department others from the list are appointed. Usually the few appointed as readers move into TAships before those below them, unless they particularly request to remain readers. This procedure continues until the new fall semester actually begins. Now and then, because of a late resignation, a reader may suddenly become a TA a couple of days before classes begin. Usually, however, TAs know their assignments in the spring before they leave for vacation.

After TAs are appointed they are required to attend a three-day preservice workshop in the fall before classes begin. These general workshops focus on such matters as determining objectives and accomplishing them, leading discussions, stating course requirements and making a syllabus, teaching the writing process, using groups effectively, using journals and other teaching resources on campus. Three days of workshops are about all that new TAs can take. They are preoccupied with finding housing and courses they will take; to expect more of them at this time just doesn't seem wise. Once school is under way, however, they are required to attend evening workshops on such matters as teaching students to revise their own papers, grading, giving lectures, and so forth. These workshops are designed to coincide with problems that may arise in their teaching as the semester progresses.

As stated earlier TAs begin by teaching an introductory writing-literature course for a year under the supervision of two faculty members (a different one each semester). They are responsible for their discussion sections, and they usually give students the course grade with considerable guidance from the faculty member. Frequently faculty members will require TAs to give a lecture on one story or book in the course, but some faculty members treat this exercise as strictly voluntary. TAs also grade the four to six papers written by students. Some faculty members spend considerable time setting up criteria for grading, and a few have the TAs write papers similar to the ones they assign in order to help them understand the difficulty of the task.

Toward the end of the second semester of the first year of teaching, TAs are required to attend workshops on teaching the elementary composition course, which almost all of them teach the following fall. They are fully responsible for the design of this course as well as for assignments and grading. Again, they are asked to write a statement about what they expect of students, and they begin working on a syllabus. They are given a 112-page manual on the course, plus dozens and dozens of handouts. They are encouraged to look at the nine tapes on teaching composition that were developed in the department. In the fall they give a copy of their syllabus to the Director of Composition and they are visited by him or a member of his staff. Many TAs continue teaching in this course for the remainder of their stay. Some go on to teach the professional writing skills course, tutor in the writing center, or work with a faculty member in a large upper-division course; the last of these is fairly rare now since enrollments have declined. Whatever their assignments they are expected to teach three sections a year. Usually they will request one section in the semester when they are doing considerable course work or are taking an exam. TAs are encouraged to hold conferences with students, but there is no departmental requirement that they do so, and some TAs seem to succeed as writing teachers very well with relatively few conferences.

After two years in the program TAs receive less frequent supervision. Most effort is put into the first year of the program, with considerable effort also going to the second year. By the third year TAs know the courses, yet they continue to work with one another or serve as experienced members of the introductory writing-literature course. TAs also serve on appropriate departmental committees such as the Composition Committee.

All TAs are appointed for four years. They receive $4,005 the first year, $4,155 the second year, $4,305 the third year, and $4,455 the fourth year. At present no good system for grievance procedures has been developed. Dismissal is rare and has occurred only because of failure to meet classes. All other teaching problems are dealt with by the Director of Composition. The departmental stand is that we should not get rid of people in trouble but should help them.

Current Problems and Future Plans

Probably some of the strengths of the Indiana University training program for TAs are the depth of faculty cooperation and the range of methods and materials. Its greatest weakness is that TAs teach primarily in composition courses and that is what they know the least about. Most of them have strong backgrounds in literature; few, however, have ever seriously studied rhetoric and composition. The few workshops on teaching composition are, by their limited nature, distortions of what one does as a writer and what one does as a writing teacher. What is needed is a course in the theory and practice of composition. Our present system seems to advocate one way to teach writing; that is a consequence of the limited knowledge TAs have about the subject and the lack of time to engage seriously in intelligent discussion of the issues involved in teaching composition. Until it is required that TAs know the subject matter of composition we will continue a patchwork, minimal approach to the course with the largest enrollment in the department.

The Composition Committee has proposed a required course on the theory, research, and teaching of college composition for all newly appointed TAs. Also, the department, in response to TA requests, is currently trying to devise grievance procedures for any problems that may arise. In addition, the department is trying to devise a way to have TAs evaluated by faculty members other than the Director of Composition and the two faculty members with whom they teach during the first year in the introductory writing-literature course. The problem with more supervision and visiting is that the department has few resources left to compensate for such efforts. Because of financial constraints the department had to cut its commitment to the visitation program run by the Composition office.

A serious problem with developing any program is to keep it vital for the new members who keep coming into it. When our program was developing there was considerable chaos, yet dozens of people helped out as new courses were developed or evaluations were needed. Now that we have a rather stable program, we find it difficult at times to get the cooperation we seek. The program has become institutionalized, and some TAs see it as another imposition—another attempt to keep them in line. We believe this attitude arises partly because TAs teach more composition these days than they did in the early seventies and they do not have the knowledge to systematically design and define their own course creations. Many follow the material given them but do not fully understand the implications underlying it. Many use any method or gimmick that comes along without determining how it fits their goals. This lack of knowledge cannot be eliminated overnight, but some knowledge through course work can put TAs back in the position of understanding and control that knowledge gives. Yet that is not all that needs to be done. Those in charge of the program must devise ways to involve TAs more—to let them see that discussion and change are possible.

Notes

[1] For a full description see Michael C. Flanigan, "Observing Teaching: Discovering and Developing the Individual's Teaching Style," *Writing Program Administration*, 3, No. 2 (Winter 1979), 17–24.

[2] See Michael C. Flanigan, "Variety, the Key to Training Programs for Faculty and Teaching Assistants," *ADE Bulletin*, No. 57 (May 1978), pp. 44–45. For free previewing of tapes write to Edgar Richardson, Audio-Visual Center, Indiana University, Bloomington, Indiana 47401.

[3] One attempt to do this in a course design is described in Michael C. Flanigan et al., "A Course in the College Teaching of English: A Cooperative Venture," *ADE Bulletin*, No. 35 (Dec. 1972), pp. 39–43. The course became difficult to administer because of all the people involved and the conflicting demands on their time.

University of Iowa, School of Letters

Richard Lloyd-Jones, with Cleo Martin and W. R. Irwin

The training and supervision of apprentice teachers at the University of Iowa are, for the most part, structurally separate from the academic programs in which the TAs are earning degrees. The freshman Rhetoric program, which includes instruction in writing, reading, and speaking, is the largest employer of graduate students. It draws from Communication and Theater Arts, English, Comparative Literature, American Studies, Afro-American Studies, Women's Studies, English Education, and the Writers' Workshop. The program has ten permanent staff members and receives its budget directly from the Office of the Dean of Liberal Arts, to whom it reports. Each academic year there are about 253 sections of twenty to twenty-two students each, not counting the writing and reading labs.

The Literature Core program, which offers the general education courses in literature, employs graduate students from the same areas except for Communication and Theater Arts and also staffs some sections with people in languages. The Core program, which is budgeted separately, reports to the director of the School of Letters. About one-seventh of 220 sections of thirty students each are taught by regular faculty on loan, and perhaps a third of the money for graduate assistants in that program is soft money appropriated by the dean as needed throughout the year.

In addition to the two large general education programs, the Writers' Workshop, American Studies, Afro-American Studies, and the English Department offer more specialized courses, which are supervised within those units. Most of these advanced programs use some classroom assistants and readers as well.

In general, graduate students enter the teaching programs after they have completed a year of graduate work. Most, therefore, have M.A. degrees and many have had teaching experience. A few are admitted without previous graduate work, provided they have had either high school teaching experience or substantial editorial and publishing experience.

Each graduate student must be nominated by the unit in which he or she is doing graduate work. Faculty committees in each graduate area put together dossiers for graduate students they wish to recommend for teaching positions. Larger units, such as English, have elaborate schemes for ranking applicants; smaller ones simply work holistically. The quality of the applicant's graduate work and her or his progress toward the degree weigh heaviest in most rankings. Financial need is irrelevant. A few are selected immediately for the specialized courses, and some are directed specifically to the Rhetoric program or to the Literature Core program. Most, however, are simply ranked and the supervisors of the teaching programs choose from the lists as they see fit. In short, teaching qualifications are the responsibility of the supervisors, although several of the doctoral programs require supervised teaching experience for the degree.

Some ground rules for appointment apply throughout the apprenticeship programs. The Director of the School of Letters apportions the available assistantships to the separate graduate units on the basis of graduate enrollments. To be sure, the Communication and Theater Arts Department takes forty percent of the appointments in the Rhetoric program, and the foreign language departments cover the particular literature options that are related to their own national language. The system of appointment is effective until about 1 June. Thereafter, the supervisors of the teaching programs are free to meld the lists, although diplomacy guides them in holding to the original distribution. Still, vacancies created by resignations or by late developing sections are filled from the general pool. Practically, this practice means people who are already on campus and know the operation firsthand are selected.

The teaching supervisors are asked to select their teaching assistants in accordance with the ranking of graduate programs. Otherwise, off-campus applicants might never get chosen, because supervisors prefer to work with people they know or at least can interview. Nevertheless, reappointments are generally favored for those graduate students who have taught well. Those reappointed are paid slightly more than those who are appointed new—the base pay for one section is now about $1,600, but the figure is adjusted upward annually by the amount of the average increase in faculty pay. Most of the new assistants receive one-third-time appointments—one class each semester— and they may opt for a third section in subsequent years. In the Rhetoric program some of those who have been particularly effective are chosen to assist with the professional development program and are given an additional increment of salary.

Some first-year graduate students may be appointed as graders or research assistants, but each graduate student is assigned to one faculty member, who supervises the work closely and is responsible for it. Although useful to the student as general indoctrination into academic responsibility, these appointments are somewhat out of the scope of the apprenticeship program. Relatively few students ever have such assignments.

The Rhetoric program offers three basic four-semester-hour courses in composition and speech; these meet four class hours a week. Two courses, paired in an eight-hour sequence, generally enroll 1,600–1,700 freshmen in sections of about twenty. Most of the remaining freshmen—about 1,500—are registered in a one-semester course that fuses the eight-hour sequence with rather heavy emphasis on the material ordinarily found in the second semester. Those students who are admitted to the accelerated course may opt to write themes and give speeches as evidence of their competence so they may receive total exemption. A few do; a few more are then assigned to a separate two-semester-hour course in either speech or writing. Most of the first-time teachers are assigned to the basic eight-semester-hour sequence. At the other end of the scale, the writing lab and the reading lab provide help for students at any point of their university career on a volunteer basis or in a two-credit-hour course. The assignment of graduate assistant teachers within this framework is based on matching the experience shown in the dossier with the demands of the courses themselves. Since much of the work is in conference, supervision by the department staff is built in. In addition, the Rhetoric program offers courses in teaching in the writing lab or the reading lab, primarily for those training to become community college teachers but also for general service to graduate students who want to teach basic students.

A new appointee in Rhetoric is provided with a general course syllabus and a substantial body of supporting suggestions, which include a list of allowable texts and suggestions for the apportioning of emphasis within the first semester's study. These materials are all available to the graduate student from the time of appointment in late spring. Since many of the appointments are made to people already on campus, a prospective graduate assistant may sit in on classes and talk to the people who are currently teaching. Many have taken graduate courses in advanced writing and the teaching of writing so they are already better than ordinarily prepared.

In addition to suggested readings, the chief preparation prior to teaching is a three-day presemester workshop conducted by the permanent staff and by experienced graduate assistants. Once the semester is started, each graduate student assistant new to the Rhetoric program is assigned to a group of ten to fourteen teachers cochaired by one of the permanent faculty members and one of the graduate student professional development leaders. These groups meet separately or together once a week to deal with the mechanics of conducting classes and with the philosophical questions of what the Rhetoric program is supposed to do for a student. Some time is allotted for joint grading of sample papers and for examining possible teaching strategies as well as the basic content of the course. In the small groups, systems for designing assignments are reviewed, previously marked papers are read and discussed, and classroom problems are analyzed. At midterm and at the end of the semester the permanent faculty member reviews each individual's teaching; this review includes reading through sample sets of papers done by representative freshmen from each class. During the second semester the intensity of the apprentice relationship is reduced and the number of meetings is cut back, but regular interaction is expected, and graduate students are drawn into program committees, which govern practically all the operational details of the program.

The Literature Core training program is less elaborate because most of those beginning their teaching in the program have extensive background in the subjects they are teaching. One basic course, Interpretation of Literature, is required of all liberal arts undergraduates. Each student is also expected to elect one additional course from a list of eight. Unless there is some particular reason for assigning a new graduate assistant to teach one of those optional courses, each is given the beginning course, a procedure that encourages the ready exchange of ideas among the teachers because they are often teaching the same texts at the same time. The contributing graduate programs—English, Comparative Literature, and American Studies—are expected to provide a number of faculty advisers so that each graduate student teacher can choose an experienced faculty member with whom to consult about teaching problems. Although there are some general staff meetings, most of the advice is given in what amounts to tutorials. Various efforts are made to distribute the advisory load equitably, but allowing the apprentice to choose inevitably means that some bunching occurs. Each faculty member is expected to make several classroom visits, to consult about assignments and paper reading, and in the end to prepare a report on the quality of the teaching completed for each of her or his advisees.

Teaching and supervision in the related programs vary according to the program. In the Writers' Workshop only those who are already experienced writers with solid publishing records are selected to teach the undergraduate poetry and fiction courses. Such graduate students are probably teaching courses they have taken in many versions before. Indeed, those chosen often have taught creative writing before. As a result, whatever counseling is needed can be carried on by incidental consultation with the regular graduate adviser or the director of the Workshop.

In American Studies, where the courses taught are primarily introductory courses in American culture, supervision is somewhat more formal, but the small size of the undergraduate program means that everybody consults about everything. The same may be said for Comparative Literature's cross-cultural courses. In Afro-American literature, the particular appointments are so much related to previous experience in music or art or other subspecialties that it is hard to separate the apprentice from the professional teacher. Indeed, most of those appointed have held faculty rank elsewhere.

These extreme cases illustrate what we hope is the general tone of the program—graduate student teachers are colleagues who happen to be relatively close to the beginning of their careers. Just as senior professors expect to help assistant professors with their scholarship and teaching, so we all expect to help the graduate assistant. We assume that rank, renown, age, or other marks of status need not be barriers. Yet, the requirement for annual reappointment makes a difference. Formal observation of a graduate student's work is essential for reappointment, and this dependence on the observations of a few makes appeal procedures, with graduate student participation, mandatory. Since the general education courses are separate from the department, it is easy to invite graduate assistants to be full partners in almost all decisions except those involving personnel equal or senior in rank. True, permanent staff members know the history; they have lived through most arguments at least once and thus have the advantage in discussion, but the votes are equal.

So far we have had more qualified graduate students wanting appointments than we have had spots to fill. Our demographers predict a drop in undergraduate enrollments, so perhaps we will still not need more assistants than we have graduate students, even though we have cut graduate enrollments. Although our graduate students in general have always taken their teaching seriously and have been relatively advanced in their studies, we seem to be getting more and more people with previous teaching experience. At least almost none are coming directly out of an undergraduate degree program. That tends to make the apprentice relationship ease into a peer relationship—one kind of experience and insight to be traded for another.

Increasing numbers of graduate students have developed serious professional and scholarly interests in teaching writing as well as in acquiring knowledge about literature. Less time needs to be spent on the platitudes of the art because the graduate students themselves are far above that level; indeed, some of the apprentices have to lead their middle-aged masters who have not considered the lower-division student for some years.

The continuing problem, however, is that mass education sometimes measures efficiency in terms of credit hours generated rather than in terms of significant learning acquired. In economic terms, writing especially, but beginning literary interpretation as well, is manual labor in an age of teaching machines. Thus it is difficult to justify the funds necessary for modest-sized sections. Still, under the guidance of a barely visible master, a new teacher needs genuine interaction with beginning college students if both are to succeed in their respective tasks of teaching and learning. The problems, though, are not for these programs of training teachers so much as for the discipline as a whole (we all need to talk to our students), but the cost issues are most acute when one adds teacher apprenticeships to the usual costs of teaching beginners. Low stipends are justified only if assistants receive learning as well as money for their service.

Kingsborough Community College, Department of English

Jack Wolkenfeld and Jane Maher

The Kingsborough internship in English is probably unique in that it is housed in a community college, which has no graduate program of its own from which to draw interns. The internship originated at a time when the job market for English teachers was much better; it continues today because of the need to train bright, young, energetic people to cope with the new problems of teaching reading and writing. The program works because members of the Kingsborough English Department are willing to devote time and energy to the program for little or no compensation. In return, the permanent faculty of the English Department have the advantage of working with graduate students who are intelligent and enthusiastic. The interns bring innovative ideas to a department that might otherwise be a less exciting place, especially in today's static job market.

The history of the program dates back to before open admissions, when Kingsborough was an ordinary New York community college, catching the overflow from its four-year-college affiliates in the City University system, especially Brooklyn College. Open admissions, guaranteeing a place in the university system for every high school graduate, brought an entirely new, less skilled student group to Kingsborough at the very time that City University, and especially Kingsborough, was in a period of significant growth. Given these factors, Kingsborough reviewed not only its curricula and teaching methods but also its methods of recruiting and training faculty.

We were willing to learn and develop methods necessary to deal with the unskilled students, and as a result we joined with the Graduate Center of City University in several federally funded summer training institutes. The institutes were designed for new teachers coming into the system as well as for experienced teachers who wanted to retrain. Because Kingsborough had a high percentage of students who needed to learn basic skills, our campus became the "field" on which the institute's participants gained "field experience." Those training at Kingsborough were becoming highly effective teachers of remedial reading and writing, but almost all of them went to other colleges after their training was completed. At about this time, funds for teacher training institutes began to dry up, so in a kind of natural progression we decided to do our own training, under our own auspices, making use of the people and the approaches of the earlier institutes.

Our first set of interns was drawn from graduate schools within the city, primarily Columbia, New York University, and City University Graduate Center, but also from other schools that offered doctorates in English. The graduate schools helped us in our selection process and provided encouragement and interest in helping us to train new teachers to face new problems. Very little training for college-level teaching existed in the New York area at the time, so we were providing a real service to the profession by helping to prepare graduate students for college teaching.

That was our basic reason for beginning the program, and it is our basic reason for continuing the program. The faculty and administration responsible for the internship also like the idea that Kingsborough is able to help its own students while helping potential teachers. The interns represent a continual stream of people who possess the freshness and readiness for work that seem to come from those who haven't been jaded by one too many faculty or budget meetings. The interns come to Kingsborough with the latest literary theories; they are still close to the experience of sitting through undergraduate classes, and they are ready to discuss and criticize as well as to learn. They are extremely effective in the classroom because they are willing to devote enormous amounts of time and energy to their students, while full-time professors are busy with their many classes and their administrative distractions. The faculty are invigorated and refreshed by the presence of the interns, because in teacher training, as in other areas, the best way to learn a subject is to teach it. Although the faculty members involved in the training and supervision of interns receive no financial compensation, they recognize the benefit of having a young, impressionable intern observe them in class for the purpose of imitation. The faculty are also rewarded through the ability to recognize immediately any adulation coming their way from the interns.

Because of this personal motivation and compensation, the organization of the program tends to be loosely structured. The general point of the program is to train doctoral candidates with little or no experience in teaching to teach reading and writing to freshmen with low skills. With that goal in mind, the faculty are highly responsive to the interns' needs and are willing to change or alter procedures if it seems necessary to do so. Because we are not funded by any outside sources, we are not restricted or limited by any preordained guidelines or funding requirements. In other words, if one thing doesn't work, we don't hesitate to try something else. This is not as arbitrary as it seems. We are dealing with interns who have only one year with us; they each have individual problems with their classes, and we find that our rather informal, flexible methods work best. Our program provides a friendly atmosphere in which the interns can freely discuss the problems that arise when motivated but inexperienced teachers encounter motivated but poorly skilled students. All our training is pragmatic and classroom-oriented, supported by some theoretical discussion in small seminars. The interns are expected to develop syllabi, to teach both reading and writing classes, and to produce usable materials of instruction. The interns are encouraged to strive to improve their students' reading and writing skills, but they are constantly reminded of the difficulty and challenge involved in trying to do so.

In short, the general objectives of the program are to increase the teaching skills of the interns, particularly in the area of remediation, and at the same time to make the interns more competitive in what is turning out to be a tight job market. In this area we seem to have been successful; in a questionnaire mailed to all former interns to obtain information for this essay, over half indicated that their teaching experience at Kingsborough had given them an advantage over other applicants for teaching positions.

To be considered for the intern program, applicants must have the master's degree, be enrolled in a program of further graduate study, intend to enter college teaching, and have the recommendation of their department. Candidates for the internship are also subjected to a lengthy interview at Kingsborough by the Director of Interns. Selection is made on the basis of the entire record, with heavy emphasis placed on the candidate's promise as a college teacher and his or her ability to profit from internship training.

The number of interns chosen per year depends on the budget and teaching needs of the department. The intern program has been in existence for ten years, with an average of six interns per year. Interns are hired for one year at Kingsborough, and they teach six hours for each of two semesters. The six hours consist of a four-hour writing class and a two-hour reading class. Interns are paid the standard adjunct rates for these six hours; in addition they receive two extra hours of compensation, for which they do additional work in preparation of teaching materials, or occasionally other work. This extra work is useful to the interns because it provides training in the production of teaching materials, plus the satisfaction of knowing that the materials may be used in the English Workshop or in other classrooms. At the present adjunct rate, with the extra two hours included, interns receive approximately $5,000 per year. After their two semesters as interns, many return to teach part-time as adjuncts. Although an intern has never been hired at Kingsborough for a full-time position, this has nothing to do with their ability as teachers; rather, it reflects the lack of available teaching positions.

The English Department is able to use its adjunct budget to fund the intern program because the Kingsborough administration supports the intern program. The only other cost for the program is minimal, in the form of one hour of released time per semester for the Director of Interns. All other work involved—supervision, observation, evaluation, interviewing, seminars, and so forth—is not compensated in time or money, making the program relatively exempt from the budget woes of City University.

Before classes even begin, interns meet with the Director of Interns several times to discuss their approach to the class. The meetings generally deal with the type of student, the syllabus, the texts, classroom approaches, criteria to be used in evaluating students, testing and counseling services, duplicating processes, audiovisual materials, and a general introduction to the campus. The interns are assigned neighboring offices, providing a place where they can share ideas and experiences. At the first meeting, interns are introduced to the Chairman of the English Department, the Director of Freshman English, the Director of the English Workshop, and the Director of the ESL courses.

Throughout the semester the interns meet to discuss and compare approaches to teaching and testing, to raise and discuss problems, and to evaluate specific materials and techniques. These meetings are informal. Sometimes the conversation is light and superficial—how long it takes to learn students' names; sometimes the interns talk about how their lives have been changed by their teaching experiences. Often, the discussions center on the dichotomy of teaching basic skills while studying sophisticated, highly developed literary ideas. Although the interns are not paid for the time spent in meetings, and despite their heavy schedules, almost every former intern indicated on the questionnaire that even more meetings would have been helpful.

These meetings provide a way to deal with the isolation the interns feel because they are separated both geographically and psychologically from their graduate schools. They must often make radical adjustments in their schedules to manage the increased workload, in addition to the commutation involved in getting from their graduate school to Kingsborough. A more serious problem is the isolation the interns sometimes feel from their fellow graduate students and their professors; their experience with low-skilled students makes them wonder about the value of their graduate work, not only in terms of future employment but in terms of personal satisfaction. One of our former interns gave this account when replying to our questionnaire:

> I had never before met, let alone taught, such eighteen-year-olds. Before coming to Kingsborough, I would have assumed that any such student was stupid. Now I no longer know what being stupid means. After my year at Kingsborough, I began to see the complexities and sorrows of these students' predicaments. I also began to think more about the relationship between present-day culture and the language skills of college students. I was temporarily overwhelmed and depressed by the difficulties of the Kingsborough teacher's task. But this depression was necessary, salutary in the long run. I decided to specialize not in literature research and teaching but rather in the teaching of writing. My experience at Kingsborough had something to do with this in that I discerned how few students there are at present for whom the study of literature makes sense.

Another intern expressed her initial frustration in having to teach such basic skills after so many years of intensive study and research:

> I was spending more time composing worksheets to teach sentence structure than I was on my own graduate work, and I was finding the shift from one level of work to another harder and harder to make. Only when I started seeing progress in my classroom did I realize how much I had in common with my students. I was struggling with Conrad; they were struggling with Freshman Composition. The point was that we were all trying to do something that was very difficult for us, and what was more important, I was able to help my students do it.

In addition to the meetings, the interns are also observed and evaluated on both an official and an unofficial basis. Because they are paid as adjuncts, the observation and evaluation are performed according to the provisions of the contract between City University and the Professional Staff Congress; they are informed of the time of the observation and are observed for a full hour. They are given a written evaluation of the observation, to which they may respond in writing. Before this official observation takes place, however, either the Director of Interns or one of the faculty members arranges an unofficial observation with each intern and discusses the observation privately, without any record. The interns often observe the classes of the faculty as well as the classes of their fellow interns, with advance permission. The interns find this a useful way to determine their own strengths and weaknesses in the classroom.

On their questionnaires, the interns noted some of the advantages of the Kingsborough internship over a teaching assistantship in the university in which they are doing their graduate work. They feel that the relationship between the intern and other faculty members is more professional; an intern is not being supervised by the same professor who is also judging him or her as a student in a seminar. Often, financial need and scholastic performance are major considerations in choosing and retaining teaching assistants; at Kingsborough, the intern can retain some autonomy—financial status is never considered (though there hasn't been an intern yet who didn't need the money) and academic status is only reviewed as an indicator of teaching potential. Kingsborough does not use its internship for any other reason than to provide training for people who want to be good teachers; graduate schools are sometimes forced to give their teaching assistantships to exceptional students who are not necessarily interested in teaching but who must have the money to continue their studies.

Interns have all stressed that the most important advantage of our program has been that the training and experience they received teaching remedial reading and writing have given them better preparation for the current job market than their peers who are participating in other programs. One of the interns noted that after Kingsborough, when he went on interviews for teaching positions, he still had to convince his future employer that he could teach, but since he no longer had to convince himself, the interview went much more smoothly. Another intern wrote about the confidence she gained at Kingsborough:

> I had been studying for years to become a teacher; I had been telling my family and friends for years that I wanted to teach, but every once in a while I would ask myself if I was just doing these things because it was too late to do something else. At Kingsborough I learned that when you walk into that classroom, either something happens or it doesn't. It's not a matter of good preparation or anything so easily defined; it's a matter of knowing for sure when a class goes so well that for the rest of your teaching career you know that you're going to remember that class and try to at least match it, maybe even do better.

The discoveries that the interns make about their students and themselves are crucial to helping them cope with the current job market. The training and exposure that the interns receive prepare them for any remedial situation and give them the actual classroom experience that so many colleges demand.

The internship program so far has received praise from all concerned.

Graduate schools like it because it gives employment to their students, which is useful both for those schools like Columbia that have extensive teacher apprentice programs and for those that do not. The interns like it because it provides them with an opportunity, all too rare these days, to get inside a classroom and teach. Kingsborough likes it because it allows the school to do something good, for the school's own students, for the interns, and for the larger academic community, at a relatively low cost. Future employers like it because it adds a touch of realism to the academic training provided to the interns at the graduate schools.

The problem is that the program is a very "soft" one; no one wants to say it is expendable, but no one can put any real money into it either. As a result, the time available for training and supervision is severely limited. Supervising faculty have to snatch time away from other responsibilities. Given these factors, the program is remarkably successful, but it is also less than it could or ought to be. Because the program is tied to the adjunct budget, the number of interns varies from year to year, causing the program to be too large at times and at other times too small. The program would have a far greater stability if it could accommodate a fixed number of interns per year.

Finally, and probably the most serious issue of them all, is the question of where it all leads, because we cannot provide jobs for the interns after they have completed their work. To some degree, the Kingsborough program has the best of both worlds on this question; we don't recruit graduate students for the profession—they already know they want to teach when they come to us. Given this, we can provide at least a few of these persistent, dedicated souls with a way of avoiding that frustration of trying to get a job without experience when experience is required to get one of the very few jobs available. But even the teaching experience gained does not compensate for the work and devotion of these interns if they are unable to find another job in the teaching profession.

We intend to go on with our program, however, on the assumption that we are being useful, at least to some extent. We bring bright, young teachers together with young students, and these young teachers help the students realize how much there is to learn. This achievement can't be ignored; concrete evidence exists in the high reading and writing scores of the interns' students. We do not expect any significant changes in the job market, but we do hope for increased coordination with the graduate departments of our interns. For one thing, we would like to work out a way of providing credit for the internship. For another, we would like to see a closer connection between the work being done in the graduate program and the internship, to eliminate to some extent the dichotomy that exists between scholarship and teaching.

At this point, it is probably appropriate to mention the occasional intern who discovers that he or she really doesn't want to teach; how lucky that person is. For those interns who are not so lucky, however, we have the small satisfaction of knowing that they were able to make discoveries about themselves and teaching through our program. All the interns who responded to our questionnaire said that they were glad to have had the opportunity to teach at Kingsborough; we were certainly glad to have them.

Marquette University, Department of English

Joseph Schwartz and Jerome Thale

The First-Year Program

A formal program for training teaching assistants goes back thirty years at Marquette. The expansion of the program into two distinct phases occurred two years ago, when, after much discussion and the provision of additional staff, the department undertook to get more full-time staff into the freshman course and to take first-year assistants—who are appointed with only the B.A.—out of teaching the freshman course. To do this we went to sections of 125 in our lower-division literature courses (Survey of British Literature, Survey of American Literature, Introduction to Literature), assigning a first-year assistant to work with the lecturer in each of the sections. The assistants are selected by a departmental committee (Department Chairman, Director of Freshman English, and Director of Graduate Studies), using transcripts, GRE scores, and letters; their duties and rights are specified in a written document from the university. All appointments are for one year, are renewable, and involve twenty hours a week service.

In the past, first-year teaching assistants, fully responsible under supervision for teaching two sections of Freshman English, found their first year—adjusting simultaneously to graduate school and to teaching—a difficult time; those pressures, combined with inexperience, sometimes made for less effective teaching than one would like. The only other way of using first-year assistants —and we must use them—was in the literature courses that fulfill general education requirements. After much discussion the department voted to use them not as discussion section leaders but as assistants in a more narrow sense. A set of guidelines, ratified by the department, carefully defines the role and workload of the teaching assistant-apprentice. Like the classical apprentice, he or she handles some of the busy work—record keeping, for example—looks on while the master does the lecturing, keeps three office hours a week to discuss both the literature content of the course and writing problems, and is heavily engaged in the grading of examinations and the two required papers in the course. Additionally, the assistant will give two or three lectures during the semester. In all, these duties (including attendance at the lectures) take probably a little less than twenty hours (teaching assistants who have moved on to teaching composition report that the workload in the first year was "not bad").

What gives substance to the term "apprentice," rather than "grader" or "aide," is a two-sided plan of instruction and supervision: a formal course directed toward the kinds of teaching activities the assistants are undertaking and the individual lecturer's continuous instruction and supervision of a teaching assistant.

The formal course, taught by the chairman of the committee that oversees the courses, is required, carries credit, is graded on a satisfactory/unsatisfactory basis, and is determinedly practical. It begins during the required orientation session before registration and will have met several times by the time regular classes start. The main emphasis of the first half of the course is on grading the type of papers assigned in these courses. Regular exercises, using three to five papers, move from the assessment of strengths and weaknesses to the writing of end comments, to the writing of marginal comments, to comparative evaluation (the approach is relativistic because in the absence of formal departmental or committee norms, each teaching assistant must adjust to the grading practices and norms of his or her lecturer) and finally reach the actual assignment of grades. Regular exercises are followed by a similar but briefer set of exercises for the evaluation of essay-type examinations. A session on conducting student conferences will be timely when the first papers are about to be returned. The latter part of the course is more reflective: discussions of the nature of student writing problems; reading Richard Larson's "Training New Teachers of Composition in the Writing of Comments on Themes," *College Composition and Communication*, 17 (1966), 152–53, and the section on grading in The Instructor's Manual for the text used in our freshman course; reading samples of the writing-about-literature books, for example, Edgar V. Roberts, *Writing Themes about Literature* (4th ed., Englewood Cliffs, N.J.: Prentice-Hall, 1977), and discussing their utility. The course concludes with an exercise in which each student plans a one-hour treatment of "Prufrock"—with a good deal of attention to the aims of the presentation (teaching assistants are pretty good at explaining and explicating, but they need to be prodded to specify the larger ends they have in mind).

The other side of the program for first-year assistants, and the one that most nearly approaches the condition of the classical apprenticeship, is the direct day-to-day working of the teaching assistant under the lecturer. The departmental guidelines governing the duties and responsibilities of each specify that the lecturer is finally responsible for all grades and is to train the teaching assistant; the guidelines also define the teaching assistant workload. A statement "On Grading Your First Set of Papers," written for the teaching assistants but given also to the lecturers, proposes a model relationship for grading in which a back-and-forth process defines the goals and expectations of a particular paper or exam: an exchange of sample papers communicates the lecturer's standards and style to the teaching assistant and gives the lecturer a sense of the teaching assistant's approach. Subsequently the review of the teaching assistant's grading gives assurance of consistency and accuracy and an evaluation of the teaching assistant's performance. Each teaching assistant is required to lecture two or three times during the semester, observed by the lecturer, who is expected to evaluate and counsel. Finally, looking forward to future assignment, the lecturer submits an end-of-the-semester evaluation.

If there is a problem, it is that while these procedures ensure fulfillment of responsibilities to our undergraduate students and make for close and continuous monitoring of teaching assistant performance, they require a great deal of work by the lecturers. The hazard is that a lecturer may not bother to do all this work and will simply leave the teaching assistant to his or her own devices. I do not think we have had this problem in our first two years—the staff is small and carefully selected—but I should personally have misgivings about such a system if the staff involved was large and one could not be assured of a high degree of motivation and responsibility. Lecturing by the teaching assistant to a large class has not been particularly successful, nor does it seem a particularly suitable preparation for teaching small classes in the second year. Still, some such lecturing seems preferable to none.

So far, this approach has worked well. Morale is high among both teaching assistants and lecturers, and the relations between lecturers and teaching assistants have been generally very good. The teaching assistants who have moved on to Freshman English find that though they are doing a great deal more than dealing with papers and examinations on literary topics, they are better prepared, surer, and more efficient.

We have at the moment no plans for any significant change, and we are not likely to consider a change unless we find some other way of using and training first-year teaching assistants.

The Second-Year Program

A formal, carefully constructed support system for TAs was begun at Marquette University in 1950. At that time Duke and Indiana, under Francis Bowman and Phillip Weiklund, respectively, were the two schools (of about 20) most active in providing leadership. The question of the kind and amount of support was a lively topic at Conference on College Composition and Communication meetings in the 1950s. The support system has changed over the years to respond to differing needs, but some of the original elements have remained. The structure recognizes the apprenticeship character of the program. This system includes a formally appointed Director of Freshman English whose administrative duties are compensated for by a substantially reduced teaching load. There is a Committee on Freshman English, made up of various ranks within the department, which is usually chaired by the director. The members of the committee undertake certain duties in conjunction with the director. After the committee has selected the common texts to be used in the course, the director submits to the committee the "Syllabus and Course Calendar" and the "Instructor's Manual." English 1 and 2, rhetoric and composition, is regarded as a single course divided into two semesters. It is required of every student enrolled in the university, except for those qualifying for advanced placement and those enrolled in the honors program. The enrollment is currently around two thousand; there are eighty sections of English 1 and 2 with twenty-five students per section.

Normally, TAs are eligible for appointments to teach two sections of English 1 after they have completed their first year in the sophomore literature program, usually in the second year of graduate study. They may be completing the M.A. or entering the Ph.D. program. The initial appointment is determined by a committee made up of the Chairman of the Department, the Director of Graduate Studies, and the Director of Freshman English. Before being assigned to teach English 1, TAs receive a second review that examines the evaluations by the teachers they assisted in the sophomore program and their performance as students in graduate courses.

The week before the semester begins, a series of staff meetings are held, attended by everyone assigned to the teaching of Freshman English. At such meetings, an orientation on the teaching of rhetoric and composition is presented. A separate session is held for TAs on grading typical freshman essays. Those assigned to teach English 1 will have taken a graduate course in teaching literature that stresses the correcting and evaluating of student writing. Concurrently with the teaching of English 1, all TAs take English 290, a graduate course in rhetoric. The emphasis of the course is more theoretical than pedagogical, since staff meetings and individual support arrangements create the opportunity for group and individualized attention to pedagogy throughout the academic year. The texts for English 290 are *The Rhetoric of Aristotle*, Plato's *Phaedrus*, and *The Province of Rhetoric*, edited by Joseph Schwartz and J. A. Rycenga (4th ed., New York: Wiley, 1965). The emphasis is on Aristotle's rhetoric and the modifications and additions made to it throughout history. Each student is expected to do a course paper on a modern rhetorician. While the "Instructor's Manual" is concerned for the most part with pedagogical problems and commonsense advice for teaching, it does include a bibliography (at times with commentary) of selected significant works in language, linguistics, rhetoric, and composition. We can no longer assume that the TA has had as a part of his undergraduate training courses in the history of the language, the structure of English, or a course in grammar. We do require the TAs to take a course in the history of the language in their first semester of teaching English 1, if they have not had such a course as an undergraduate. Over the past ten years we have noticed appalling deficiencies in entering graduate students in their knowledge of grammar, syntax, and so forth.

TAs are not obliged to pick their own texts or to prepare course calendars; this material is common to all sections of the course. They are assigned to teach two sections of English 1 (one would be better), meeting six periods and preparing three lessons a week. They are obliged to keep three office hours per week. There is an average of eight themes per semester, most limited to five hundred words. We try to plan for a realistic total of twenty hours per week devoted to teaching duties: preparing for class, meeting classes, correcting papers, holding office hours, attending staff meetings, and having individual conferences with the experienced staff member to whom the TA is assigned.

Since the texts are chosen by the Committee on Freshman English, which helps prepare the syllabus, it is possible for the Director of Freshman English to prepare well in advance of the semester an "Instructor's Manual" (about 50 pages), available to everyone teaching the course but directed specifically to the teaching assistant and the new instructor. It covers the following general topics: teaching Freshman English at Marquette University, housekeeping details, reading and grading themes, commenting on the course calendar. The TA and the new instructor are made aware of the philosophy and goals of the course, given some general advice concerning pedagogy, and told about the details of departmental routine. The longest section is a day-by-day commentary on the course calendar, defining the goals for each unit of the course and suggesting alternative methods of covering the material. Five staff meetings are held each semester dealing with a variety of mixed topics: "how to teach" presentations; assigning, reading, and grading themes; theoretical matters; responses to especially important books and articles, standard or contemporary. Members of the staff, including TAs, participate in presenting these topics, although at times an expert in testing, or logic, or some other field may be invited to give a presentation.

Each TA is assigned to an experienced member of the department, a member of the Committee on Freshman English, or someone concurrently teaching the course. This mentor may have one or two TAs per semester. Themes 4 and 6 are reviewed in depth by the mentor at scheduled conference times. The mentor visits at least one class (most of the time two) and discusses the class with the TA. The mentor also acts as a resource person for the TA throughout the semester. Each TA has a different mentor each semester on the principle that various responses are better than a single one.

The Director of Freshman English visits the classes of all TAs every semester, writes an evaluation of the classroom performance, and uses that written document as a basis for a conference with each TA. The director also reviews the grades given on each theme by every TA, countersigns the final grade sheet for each section of English 1 and 2 taught by the TAs, and arranges for each TA to have a class taped through the facilities of the Media Resource Center. The teaching assistant may view the tape alone or may view it with the mentor. TAs submit to the director written analyses of their tape, an exercise meant to emphasize the problem of perceiving oneself in relation to the perception of others. The taping is done only once, unless circumstances warrant requesting a repeat. The university requires that Student Evaluation Forms be completed every semester for every course; this includes the classes of TAs. The forms turned in at the end of the course by the students are discussed by the director with the teaching assistant every semester. The staff, including TAs, engage in an exchange-of-themes grading exercise for one theme in the first semester. Care is taken to assign an experienced teacher, not the TA's mentor, as the partner, for the purposes of making the staff aware of the diligence needed to make grading as equitable as it can be when thirty-five different persons are teaching the same course. While both readers grade the theme, the commentary and grade for this theme is given by the "visiting instructor." Disputes concerning grades are settled between the two graders before the papers are handed back to the students.

Any written reports are regarded as in-house documents that do not become part of the TA's public dossier. When it comes time to seek formal letters of recommendation for the public dossier, the TA can select from various staff members who by then know the TA's work well. The full-time members of the staff who engage in supervision are not compensated by salary or reduced load. The department has agreed that the induction of apprentices into the profession is a major responsibility carried out in the normal course of our work. The minimal formal supervision contacts per year with the teaching assistant, outside of staff meetings, are three class visitations, four theme conferences, a theme-grading exchange, fifteen theme-grading reviews, a final conference, and two semester grade reviews.

A Materials Resource Center stocked with books, texts, and teaching materials is available to the TA. Some of these materials are specifically mentioned or described in the "Instructor's Manual."

The TA is given a nine-month contract, yearly, that spells out the duties, identifies the stipend, and describes the tuition-free fringe benefit. Like all other students, the graduate student has available various university benefits. Grievances are handled by the Director of Freshman English, the Committee on Freshman English, and the Chairman of the Department. The TA does not have faculty status, but participation in the governance of the department occurs through a system of elections by the Association of English Graduate Students for representatives to departmental meetings, the Committee on

Freshman English, the Committee on Sophomore English, and the Committee on Graduate Studies.

Current problems in achieving the goals of this program for Freshman English persistently include the TA's lack of experience. The tension between training the apprentice and not shortchanging the tuition-paying freshman is always present. Recently, we have noted a severe lack of background knowledge of language and grammar. There is almost no undergraduate training in logic and ethics and, far more important, no training in rhetoric. The TA's training and interests are almost exclusively in English literature—very little in literature in other languages. Particularly noticeable in the last five years has been the cultural phenomenon of carelessness, casual attention to duties, missing classes without sufficient reason, returning themes late, and so on. There is a tendency on the part of the TA to regard grades as a confirmation of the personal and social relationship of instructor and student rather than as a measure of the student's performance in a given subject. Naturally, the result has been grade inflation. Our efforts recently have been directed quite vigorously toward impressing the TA with a sense of professionalism. In summary: lack of knowledge of the discipline being taught and a misunderstanding of what being professional means are the major problems we currently confront.

Future plans include a consideration of the ways in which the two pedagogically oriented graduate courses can be more carefully unified to make the TA's apprenticeship more coherent. When these courses are taught by the same person, that unity of intent may be arrived at naturally. Plans to have both graduate courses taken by the TA *before* teaching English 1 and 2 are under consideration. Since we deal with a limited number of TAs, we may develop extensively the working relationship between the TA and the mentor. This plan is necessarily self-limiting because of the number of experienced teachers who volunteer to participate and who have the competence to be a mentor in rhetoric and composition. We intend to hold firmly to our commitment to have firm philosophical underpinnings for the course, in contrast to the tendency to tread water in thinking about the freshman course or to regard it as an ad hoc solution to a problem that may surface at a given time. This commitment means constant attention to continuing and improved ways of educating the whole staff in a discipline that few are prepared in any formal way to teach.

University of Michigan, Department of Near Eastern Studies

Raji M. Rammuny

The Teacher Training (TT) program in the Department of Near Eastern Studies (NES) started in the ·fall semester of 1971 as an outgrowth of the department's reorganization of its educational program. The TT program as it was originally designed included a Preteaching Conference and NES Teacher Training Methods Course 837. The acquisition of a small grant from the Danforth Fund in 1973 enabled us to add to the program student teaching, involvement of Senior Teaching Assistants (STAs), Videotape Lesson Demonstrations (VLDs), teacher training seminars, evaluation procedures, and the development of a Handbook for NES Graduate Teaching Assistants (GTAs). Most recently, a Bibliography on Foreign Language Learning and Teaching has also been added.

Preteaching Conference

NES GTAs, Teacher Trainees (TTs), and Student Teachers (STs) attend a one-day conference that is normally held prior to the start of classes in the fall semester. The conference is run by instructors in charge of elementary and intermediate language classes with the assistance of some experienced GTAs. Topics discussed at the conference include a description of the structure of NES and its policies and regulations with regard to students and GTAs; brief group discussions of the courses to be taught, the instructional materials to be used or designed, and the teaching procedures suggested to handle them; lectures on some aspects of teaching; demonstration lessons; distribution and discussion of samples of tests; language lab tour; and a display of language textbooks. The conference aims at providing TAs with some basic training and orientation needed for their assignments.

Teacher Training Methods Course 837

Students taking this course are of two types: TTs who have completed a three-year study of a Near Eastern language and/or achieved mastery of the language of their specialization and graduate STs who are willing to offer assistance and guidance to elementary and intermediate students who need extra help in their language studies. TTs are required to do all the work described in the outline below, for five credit hours. STs undergo minimum training and therefore enroll in this course for two credit hours only. (Further details are given in the next section.) The following is the Methods Course outline:

1. Attendance at a preteaching conference.
2. Classroom observation (10–12 class sessions).
   TT observes actual teaching in classroom, discusses observations with the Course Instructor (CI) or the Senior Teaching Assistant (STA) in charge of the course, and then draws up lesson plans of the teaching observed with the help and guidance of CI/STA.
3. Teaching practice.
   a. 15- to 40-minute sessions (4 weeks—once a week).
      (1) CI/STA guides TT in preparing a lesson plan for teaching pronunciation, observes TT trying it out in the classroom, and confers with TT after class about the TT's teaching.
      (2) TT practices teaching a basic text of a lesson, using a lesson plan. CT/STA does the same as above.
      (3) TT explains grammar to class, using a lesson plan as in (1) above.
      (4) TT conducts a drill session, using a lesson plan as in (1) above.
   b. 50-minute sessions (2 weeks—once a week).
      TT teaches one class session per week, following an outline of the section(s) of the lesson to be presented to the class. CI/STA observes the teaching and confers with the TT immediately after class.

    c. Whole-lesson sessions (5 weeks—once a week).
        TT teaches a complete lesson per week following same procedure as above.

4. Grading and test experience.
    During the period of practice teaching, TT receives training in grading assignments and tests. TT is given samples of old quizzes, tests, and and exams to look at and discuss with CI/STA. Papers and tests graded by TT should be given to CI to be checked before they are returned to students. Under CI/STA's guidance, TT prepares and grades some of the quizzes and tests given to the class.

5. Preparation of supplementary teaching materials.
    TT is given some responsibility for collecting and preparing some of the supplementary cultural and enrichment materials required by the course.

6. Exchange of visits.
    a. TT visits CI/STA's classes as well as other language classes in NES and other foreign language departments on the campus in order to gain insight into various approaches and techniques that are in practice. TT writes short reports on the visits and discusses observations with CI/STA.
    b. CI/STA attends all TT's classes and discusses matters related to teaching.

7. Assigned readings.
    Throughout the course, CI/STA refers TT to a bibliography including articles in professional journals and books on foreign language learning and teaching. TT is free to read and to suggest new materials to be added to the bibliography.

8. Evaluation.
    A file is kept on CI's observations of TT's classes as well as the meetings and discussions between them. This file serves as a good source from which evaluation of TT's teaching experience and competence can be drawn.

9. Group meetings.
    All TTs, STs, and CIs/STAs meet together once a week in order to exchange teaching experiences, discuss and analyze teaching problems of common and general nature and make a coordinated attack on them, and handle unusual class situations.

Student Teaching

This innovative method of teaching aid was suggested by NES student representatives on the Curriculum Committee. It reflects the desire of some of our advanced graduate students to participate, on a tutorial basis, in offering assistance and guidance to elementary and intermediate students who need extra help in their language course work. STs who have not taken NES Teacher Training Methods Course 837 are required to undergo minimum training in teaching by enrolling in the course for two hours only. Their training involves an hour of class visitation or tutoring and another hour for discussion of teaching procedures and problems related to their tutoring or reading assignments.

    At the beginning, STs tutor one or two students, but later they are given the opportunity to tutor groups of three to five students. The class is divided into small groups of three to five students and STs are asked to teach them during the class period. Sometimes an ST is asked to teach the whole class when the instructor in charge of the course finds this to be possible.

It should be noted here that STs' work is always coordinated and supervised by course instructors and/or STAs in order to ascertain problems and needs of both STs and their students. For this purpose STs keep records of all things that happen during the tutoring period, such as problems discussed, supplementary materials and procedures used in handling students' questions, students' reactions and motivation, and other related matters. Reports obtained from the STs so far include sessions on a wide range of topics: grammatical explanations, speed reading, writing and spelling problems, and questions related to the nature and culture of the target language under question.

This cooperative student teaching experiment has been very useful. It has helped in creating respect and cooperation between our graduate and undergraduate students as well as between STs and course instructors and/or STAs, increasing student participation and preparation for teaching, and personalizing teaching experience by giving more attention to the individual student.

Senior Teaching Assistants

A key feature of our TT program is the involvement of STAs, who are selected on the basis of their excellence in training and competence in teaching as GTAs. The availability of STAs in our program has been found crucial in order to develop a sense of professionalism in them, by providing them with the opportunity of coordinating the preteaching workshop, the TT seminars, and STs' work. We consider this type of experience essential to STAs before they graduate and assume their responsibilities as full instructors. The following are some of the major services rendered by STAs:

> Help new TTs, STs, and GTAs collect and/or design teaching materials and tests. We feel that there is a great need for this type of assistance and training, especially since most language teachers nowadays are being required to do their own programs and course outlines.
>
> Accompany TTs, STs, and GTAs to the language lab in order to explain and/or demonstrate to them the importance and significance of the language lab in the teaching-learning process.
>
> Discuss with TTs, STs, and GTAs teaching problems and other matters related to classroom teaching during the TT seminar meetings or whenever such problems arise.
>
> Assist TTs, STs, and GTAs in making and grading tests and in designing lesson plans and implementing them.

Videotape Lesson Demonstrations (VLD)

Another important feature of our TT program is the production of videotapes and video cassettes based on natural classroom teaching done by some of our faculty members, STAs, and experienced GTAs who are involved in teaching our various elementary and intermediate language courses. The VLDs range between fifteen to thirty minutes in length and cover a selected variety of teaching-learning aspects: drilling, grammatical explanation, reading and writing, discussion of reading texts, and review sessions.

We usually use some portions of these VLDs in our TT seminars to discuss their contents. We also schedule selected parts of them for our preteaching conferences to give our new GTAs, TTs, and STs the chance to view some of our teaching procedures before they start teaching classes.

The main purposes of VLDs are to coordinate methods and procedures used in our different language classes by selecting those methods that, in our opinion, have proved effective, to offer GTAs, TTs, and STs the opportunity to gain new insights in teaching, and to promote intercommunication and cooperation among our language sections.

Teaching Training Seminars

We have experienced two types of TT seminars: impromptu seminars to discuss and handle teaching problems, especially those encountered by TTs and STs, and weekly seminars during which VLDs are replayed and discussed and issues concerning tutoring and reading assignments are analyzed and straightened out.

These TT seminars have enabled us to discuss and analyze common teaching issues and to derive some valuable observations:

> Except for grammatical explanations, constant use of the target language in class should become a regular practice.
> One must be careful not to overemphasize structures for beginning students; rather, one must ask them to accept limited explanations with the assurance that more comprehensive ones will be forthcoming in the second year.
> A lesson plan is very important in organizing the teaching-learning process; therefore, a beginning teacher is encouraged to prepare a detailed lesson plan in the first weeks of teaching and to use outlines later.
> There is no single method or approach to be followed in teaching. The best approach is a blend of many methods and techniques derived from success in actual classroom experience.
> The motive for trying new techniques or ideas in teaching should come from the teacher; it should not be imposed by others.
> Weekly tests or quizzes are recommended in language classes in order to review what has been learned and detect students' problems.
> It is helpful to use supplementary cultural and enrichment readings to reinforce vocabulary and grammatical structures learned in class and to correct errors made by students, including errors involving stress and intonation.
> Freedom of expression through practice of the vocabulary and grammatical patterns learned should be attempted as early as possible. For this purpose periodic short written compositions, to be read aloud and discussed in class, are recommended.
> Emphasis should be placed on both oral and written work, starting with the elementary level. Oral work, however, should precede writing.
> Translation drills by students in the target language have been found effective in review sessions.

Evaluation Procedures

We have developed two evaluation forms: one for the evaluation of GTAs' teaching in particular and the other for course evaluation. The two forms have been designed cooperatively by a group of students, GTAs, and instructors representing NES language classes.

The approach followed in our evaluation forms has a different outlook toward evaluating teaching and teaching personnel. First, the criteria included take into consideration all aspects of the teaching-learning environment: the student, the GTA, the instructor, the textual material, and the administrator. Second, the areas to be evaluated have been clearly discussed and defined by all the parties concerned, thus removing any suspicion that may be thought of concerning the practicality of the process or its constructive aims. Third, the results obtained from evaluation are used by instructors and GTAs in revising or improving some of their teaching practices and techniques, especially those needing attention and study. Another outcome of this evaluation is the availability of some basic information that NES Department uses in rehiring or promoting GTAs.

The following guidelines have been suggested for the implementation of GTAs' evaluation and course evaluation.

1. GTA Evaluation
   a. That GTAs be informed at the beginning of the term that their classes will be visited from time to time by NES staff members.
   b. That an effort be made to arrange a mutually convenient time for the evaluation visit and to acquaint the observer with the overall context of the lesson to be observed.
   c. That each evaluation visit be followed by a meeting between GTA and observer in order to discuss and clarify the reactions of the observer and suggest areas needing improvement.
   d. That each Class Visit Report (CVR) be signed by observer and GTA visited.
   e. That GTA's disagreement with the contents of the CVR be noted in a written statement to be submitted by GTA representing the differences in opinion. Such a statement should be attached to CVR before it is placed in GTA's folder.
   f. That copies of the CVR be kept with observer, GTA, and in GTA's folder.
   g. That NES Teacher Training Committee review all evaluation reports of GTAs in order to make recommendations for rehiring and promotions and to resolve conflicts resulting from differences in opinion between GTAs and visitors.
2. Course Evaluation
   a. That Course Evaluation (CE) forms be distributed to all language sections at the end of each semester.
   b. That each class or section taught by more than one person be given enough copies of the CE forms in order to provide for evaluation of all the teaching staff involved.
   c. That students be told to fill out CE forms in class and hand them to NES administrative secretary.
   d. That all CE forms be reviewed, first, by the NES Administration for information related to the improvement of curriculum and teaching performance and, second, by course instructors and their GTAs in order to collect information concerning their teaching.
   e. That information gathered from CE be used the following semester for the improvement of methods and instructional quality as well as for clarification of some points or issues that the students have raised.

Handbook for TAs

A major aspect of our TT program has been preparation of a handbook that includes some clear guidelines related to department policies and regulations with respect to role, responsibilities, rights, and selection of GTAs; NES Teacher Training Methods Course outlines; sample lesson plans; sample tests; samples of Class Visit Report and Course Evaluation form; some observations for NES prospective language teachers from the teaching seminar; and Reading List on Language Teaching and Learning. The *Handbook for Graduate Teaching Assistants* may be obtained by writing to Department of Near Eastern Studies, 3074 Frieze Building, Ann Arbor, Michigan 48109.

State University of New York, Binghamton, Department of English

Paul E. Szarmach

The Department of English at the State University of New York at Binghamton has established an Instructional Training Program to train and develop two-year college, four-year college, and university teachers of literature and composition. The following description provides concise information on the nature of the program.

History

The present form of the Instructional Training Program operates under the 30 November 1972 memorandum issued by the chancellor at that time, Ernest L. Boyer, and entitled "Guidelines for the Evaluation of Graduate Programs." Having accepted the recommendations of two study committees on a number of points including teaching, the chancellor wrote:

> All M.A. and Ph.D. programs should develop, and submit to Deans, affirmative action procedures for the training of graduate students in the effective teaching of the discipline. Satisfactory demonstration of mastering this teaching skill should be as much of a requirement for the degree as is mastery of the discipline and demonstration of research capability.

The SUNY Central Administration left each individual campus to determine its own course of action, and the SUNY-Binghamton higher administration in turn let each graduate department establish its own training program according to the requirements and needs of the individual disciplines. The Department of English, however, had anticipated this directive, for since the inception of its graduate program in 1965 the department had had an evolving college teacher training program. The Boyer memorandum in effect gave constitutional status to what had been the department's practice.

But the concern for college teaching in the department has an even more fundamental source. Harpur College, the undergraduate arts and sciences unit of SUNY-Binghamton, began as one of two liberal arts colleges in SUNY. Harpur College has retained the traditional liberal arts values to the extent that it is still one of the most selective public four-year colleges in the United States, and, certainly in the Department of English, successful teaching is a necessary condition for promotion and tenure. Good students and demanding professional peers expect excellent teaching from every faculty member. Indeed, no department in SUNY can equal the number of excellent and distinguished teachers cited by the chancellor in his Awards in Teaching competition. This traditional departmental commitment to teaching has been reinforced by the local university administration, which in 1979 started an annual Teaching Improvement Program featuring panels, seminars, and information sessions for newly arrived TAs in all departments and schools. Perhaps inspired by the perception that good teaching will yield good enrollments, the entire SUNY-Binghamton campus continues the earlier traditions of Harpur College. The Instructional Training Program of the Department of English, therefore, exists on a campus where faculty and administration together value good teaching and by their professional commitment give example to prospective teachers.

Objectives and Purposes

In order to carry out the chancellor's directive requiring teaching mastery in the discipline of the degree, the Department of English has established the Instructional Training Program for its M.A. and Ph.D. students. The program seeks to give a theoretical introduction to the art of college teaching and practical experience in that art. Successful completion of the program is a requirement for either graduate degree.

Organization of the Program

The Instructional Training Program is an administrative unit within the Department of English; its director reports to the Chairman of the Department and works in close concert with the Director of Graduate Studies, the Director of Undergraduate Studies, the Codirectors of the Expository Writing Program, and the Director of the Two-Year College Teaching Program. The director's main responsibilities are to schedule the assignments of all students on graduate stipend and to monitor the performance of all graduate assistants. When requested by a graduate student to do so, the director writes a letter for the student's placement file that describes and assesses the student's performance in the Instructional Training Program. The director serves generally throughout the academic year without extra compensation but receives a one-course reduction per year (the standard teaching load is five courses per year) and compensatory time after the term of service.

No other faculty are regularly involved in the direct functioning of the Instructional Training Program. The director asks colleagues to visit the classes of graduate assistants teaching their own courses in literature. These visitations, rotated among the faculty, are part of the general service obligation to the department. The codirectors of the Expository Writing Program are the direct supervisors of the graduate students who teach and assist in courses in writing. Faculty who teach literature courses requiring assistants or who are assisted in research, publication, and other projects supported by the department are obviously also direct supervisors. It is assumed that direct supervisors are counselors and advisers as well as evaluators.

All graduate students who are on stipend must participate in the Instructional Training Program. In recent years the total complement of M.A. and Ph.D. students on stipend has been about sixty. There is an annual turnover of about twenty-five to thirty as a result of graduations, resignations, and completion of terms of service. Stipends vary according to seniority and experience, the average being $3,500 and the range $3,300 to $4,000. Typically, a full tuition waiver accompanies the standard stipend. The total aid package then averages over $5,000. Assistantships are given for one-year periods; M.A. candidates are eligible for a second year, while doctoral candidates are eligible for a second and third year. Graduate stipends are the only direct costs of the Instructional Training Program.

Those students not on stipend are also, by force of the chancellor's directive, participants in the Instructional Training Program. Except for students in the Two-Year College Teaching Program, where interning at a two-year college for a semester and English 394 are specific requirements, the students not on stipend demonstrate mastery through success in English 389.

Functioning of the Program

To describe more concretely the functioning of the program it would be convenient to follow the likely career of an M.A. candidate entering in the fall of 1980.

After a student accepts a graduate assistantship, the Director of Instructional Training Program reviews the student's file to determine the student's general interests and abilities. The director attempts to match the student with the teaching needs of the department as established by the May preregistration of upperclassmen or perhaps by the July preregistration of freshmen. The student receives an assignment as an assistant in an appropriate course or teaching program where a regular faculty member serves as direct supervisor. When the M.A. student registers in September, the Director of Graduate Studies registers the student in English 389, Teaching of College Composition and Literature, unless prior study qualified the student for exemption. The student also receives an invitation to attend the Writing Program's workshop-seminar for graduate assistants and the university's Teaching Improvement Program. When the department establishes the spring schedule in late December, the progress of the student in English 389 and in the teaching assignment, along with the teaching needs of the department, may lead to another position as an assistant or to an assignment as a "teacher of record," that is, the instructor responsible for course organization and for course grades, in the Writing Program. If the student receives a second assignment as an assistant, then it is relatively certain, assuming a successful performance, that in the second year of the M.A. he or she will be a teacher of record. Once a student becomes a successful teacher of record, the student's assignments will alternate between the Writing Program and the Freshman-Sophomore Literature Program. It is departmental policy that graduate assistants do not serve as teachers of record in major or upper-level courses.

Students with special abilities or interests may receive assignments in support of the department's research or publications programs. These students are considered to be in the Instructional Training Program for administrative purposes. As a general rule such assignments may not exceed fifteen hours a week. Doctoral-level students who come with teaching experience generally do not take English 389; they usually serve as teachers of record in their first term of residency.

Since the M.A. in Two-Year College Teaching (TYCT) is a variation on the traditional M.A., students in this program have a concomitant variation in their participation in the Instructional Training Program. These students must take English 394 and must spend one semester as an intern at a two-year college. The teaching internship duty is the supervised teaching of one complete course. While at SUNY-Binghamton, TYCT students generally receive assignments in the Writing Program and not in the Freshman-Sophomore Literature Program. They also receive assignments as tutors in composition, especially with the Writing Center.

It will be useful here to elaborate on the component parts of the Instructional Training Program:

English 389: Teaching of College Composition and Literature. From semester to semester the emphasis and content of this course vary to some degree, but the course description for fall 1980 gives an accurate picture of recent faculty thinking about the "theory" of teaching:

> A workshop approach to the teaching of composition and literature to college students. During the course of the semester each student will: (1) contribute one long review article to an anthology "Ideas on the Teaching of Composition and Literature"; (2) edit for publication one of the submitted articles; (3) construct a detailed syllabus for his or her own version of Rhetoric 110 (Writing I); (4) construct a detailed syllabus for her or his own version of English 120, Introduction to Literary Analysis; (5) conduct a fifteen-minute class on some phase of composition assigned by the instructor; (6) conduct a fifteen-minute class on a poem or short story assigned by the instructor.

The fall 1979 version of this course featured more intensive work on the "new rhetoric" and sought to familiarize students with current developments in teaching writing as process. Whatever the variations in theoretical content, English 389 is the preparation for participation in the Department's Writing Program. This program consists of three levels of courses: Writing I, for students with special or second-language problems; Writing II, for students who need to develop writing skills; and Writing III, for students who wish to polish writing skills. The Writing Program also sponsors a Writing Center, where undergraduates may receive tutorial help. The graduate student who successfully completes English 389 is ready to participate in any part of the Writing Program.

English 391: Teaching Practicum. The department has created this course to monitor the teaching activities of graduate assistants. Those students on stipend who are not taking English 389 get variable credit on a satisfactory/unsatisfactory grading basis as their supervised participation in the Instructional Training Program.

English 394: Practical Introduction to Teaching in the Two-Year College. This course, taught by the Broome County Community College English Department faculty, is required for those students in the M.A. in Two-Year College Teaching Program. It exposes SUNY-Binghamton graduate students to the special problems of teaching community college students: finding appropriate texts, motivating two-year college students, working in an environment in which community service and educational technology assume special importance. The course is a prerequisite to the teaching internship program in the two-year college.

Orientation Seminar in Rhetoric. Given for the first time in September 1979, in response to the interests of TAs, this seminar provides in brief the theory and background in teaching writing as well as an introduction and orientation to the scope, structure, and intention of the Writing Program at SUNY-Binghamton. The codirectors of the Writing Program discuss the general philosophy of the program and the general guidelines under which the Writing Program operates. The codirectors provide information on the three specific courses in the program, text selection, course pacing, grades and grading, current methodologies, and the functioning of the campus Writing Center. Returning graduate assistants receive an update on any changes in the Writing Program or the Freshman-Sophomore Literature Program.

Teaching Improvement Program Seminar. The Office of the President inaugurated this seminar series in September 1979 to introduce graduate assistants to the science and art of college teaching. The seminars provide basic information on academic procedures, suggestions and advice on the responsibilities of college teaching, and information on local academic customs and regulations. The program begins with two days of meetings during the preregistration period and continues with a series of Monday afternoon meetings during the fall. Faculty and staff from various departments and units participated throughout the entire semester.

Faculty supervision. The Instructional Training Program cannot work unless faculty supervise their assistants. The codirectors of the Writing Program meet regularly with their assistants in both group and individual meetings. They advise on all aspects of course organization and presentation, observe and evaluate the progress of their assistants, and render a formal, final report on each assistant at the end of the semester.

Faculty supervision in the Freshman-Sophomore Literature Program tends to be more variable because assignments differ. Teaching assistants who are teachers of record must confer directly with the Director of Undergraduate Studies, who advises them on course content and departmental expectations. Teachers of record teach their own courses, set the standards, and assign the grades; they are virtually independent. The Director of Instructional Training, who recommends assistants for assignments as teachers of record, ensures that they are visited at least once each semester by a regular faculty member, who in effect serves as an external reviewer of the course and its progress. The faculty observer files a class visitation report.

Faculty members whose lecture courses include discussion sections perform functions analogous to those described above. They meet regularly with their assistants to discuss course planning, establish grading standards, and monitor course progress. They are urged but not required to ask their assistants to offer at least one lecture before a large group. Faculty do not place unreasonable burdens on their assistants; all duties take on the average no more than about fifteen hours a week to perform. Since the faculty lecturer establishes course content, sets standards, and assigns final grades, TAs do not have the independence of teachers of record.

Faculty whose courses do not include regular discussion sections have less opportunity to involve assistants in the teaching process of their courses, but they are expected to use the assistants as more than mere graders and administrative assistants.

Graduate assistant participation. The Instructional Training Program contains no provision in its formal structure for graduate assistant participation in governance and administration. The department's bylaws, however, give three seats on the Graduate Policies Committee to graduate students, whose election is conducted by the English Graduate Organization. The Graduate Policies Committee is the committee of original jurisdiction for all general matters concerning the Instructional Training Program. Personal grievances of whatever kind would be first registered with the Director of the Instructional Training Program; the avenue of successive appeal is the Director of Graduate Studies, the Chairman of the Department, and finally the Provost for Graduate Studies and Research. The English Graduate Organization, which is not a bargaining unit, represents the views of the entire group of assistants.

Both in letter and in spirit the department has sought to view its graduate assistants as professional associates. For example, one of the codirectors of the Writing Program is working on a committee of rhetoric teachers, most of whom are graduate assistants, to develop curricular materials based on the idea of "writing as process."

Current Problems and Difficulties

Without creating an overbearing bureaucratic superstructure the department has organized a training program for teachers that intends to preserve and maintain the continuing tradition of the humanities. The problems of the program are essentially human ones: encouraging faculty to supervise conscientiously and motivating graduate students to put forth their best efforts. While the Writing Program continues to be the most effectively supervised, the Freshman-Sophomore Literature Program sometimes suffers from the diversity of faculty commitment to conscientious supervising. It is, of course, debatable whether more and more bureaucratic control will ever achieve the true end: exciting, interesting, and well-taught classes. As for motivating graduate students, the best form of academic leadership has always been professional example. The fundamental problem in graduate staffing seems equally eternal: the admission and retention of the best students. SUNY-Binghamton lags behind somewhat in the financial generosity of its stipend, but the department attempts to compensate by limiting the teaching load to one section a term.

Future Plans and Prospects

At the present time there are no plans for any large-scale revision of the Instructional Training Program or its constituent parts. It is likely that the Writing Program, and its theoretical complement, English 389, will continue with minor adjustments and further refinement. It is probable that the Director of Undergraduate Studies will seek to involve more faculty more regularly in the Writing Program and in the Freshman-Sophomore Literature Programs. The department at SUNY-Binghamton has about as many majors as it had in 1974 and more students overall than it has ever had—all in defiance of national trends. The demand on teaching resources for the nonmajor program will have to be answered by more faculty participation rather than by an increase in the number of graduate assistants. To accommodate the numbers of students, it may be more prudent to rely even more on large lecture courses, thus reducing the number of small classes taught by graduate assistants independently as teachers of record. Whatever the immediate solutions to the problem of large enrollments, the problem proves the axiom that good teaching leads to good enrollments. Better this *felix culpa* than its radical alternative.

Ohio State University, Basic Foreign Language Programs

Gerard L. Ervin

For many years the training of foreign language teaching assistants, or Graduate Teaching Associates (GTAs), as they are formally known at Ohio State University, was an intradepartmental matter.[1] Most of the language departments formally appointed a GTA supervisor, but that was about the extent of the uniformity. Some departments offered graded, formal teaching methods courses that the GTAs were required to take; others required attendance at weekly meetings during the term for coordination and consultation with other GTAs and the supervisor but did not give any formal recognition to this activity as course work. Some required new GTAs to arrive on campus a few days early in order to attend an orientation and training session; others were satisfied to invite their apprentice teachers to a general departmental meeting a day or two before classes started.

Recently, however, the departments have begun to recognize economic and professional advantages in relinquishing some of their autonomy in favor of a combined effort. Coordinated centrally, this effort allows each department considerable latitude to prepare its GTAs in a way that respects each language program's goals and teaching approaches. Thus, the GTA training program has evolved into a two-phase format: a preservice workshop, run cooperatively by the departmental GTA supervisors and with provisions for individual sessions by language group, and an in-service supervised teaching component, run separately by each language's GTA supervisor for his or her supervisees.

By and large, the faculty tend to view this program as a training course to help the GTAs teach their courses. Some departments, however, have begun to accept the program as an integral part of the preparation of future teacher-scholars, and at least one department chairperson directly attributes a striking recent increase in undergraduate student retention in his department's elementary language courses to the participation of his GTAs in the workshop.

Background of the Program

The present format of the GTA training program had its beginnings in the fall of 1978, when the Department of German and the Department of Slavic and East European Languages and Literatures decided jointly to offer a two-week, preterm intensive training course for their GTAs. The new course met all day for two full weeks, and was required of all new GTAs in these two departments. There were two faculty members and twenty GTAs. The GTAs were paid and received graduate credit for their participation. The course was taught by one faculty member from each department and, judging from the participants' evaluations and subsequent teaching performance, was quite successful.

There was much room for improvement, to be sure: the first running was theory- and lecture-oriented, with some practical sessions of peer teaching included so that the GTAs could try to apply the theory. Nevertheless, there was little doubt that the course was long overdue.

In the fall of 1979 a number of changes took place in the course. Most striking, perhaps, was its expansion, by demand, to include faculty and incoming GTAs from other language departments: in this second running there were five assigned faculty and fifty-four students in the course, representing five departments and eight languages, both classical and modern. The present report is based on this most recent program.

Objectives and Purposes of the Program

The program has two distinct phases: the preservice workshop followed by in-service supervised teaching. The dual purposes of the program are also worth reiteration: first, the immediate concern that GTAs be prepared to teach the courses to which they will be assigned (essentially a matter of training); second, the long-range goal of beginning to develop within the GTAs the professional attributes and attitudes toward teaching that they will carry with them throughout their careers (a matter of education). There is also a third important by-product of the preterm format: GTAs who are new to the city and to the university become acclimated to both without the added pressures of teaching.

The objective of the "training" phase, as given on the syllabus for the 1979 preterm workshop, was straightforward: "classroom teaching survival skills." The faculty agreed that this would be a skill-building course, grounded in theory but centered on practice. The target audience would be new GTAs, most of whom had neither prior experience nor training in teaching and almost all of whom would, immediately after the course, be assigned to teach beginning sections in their respective languages. The faculty agreed that no attempt would be made to train the students in a single orthodox teaching style; indeed, for many activities care was taken to mix the students and supervisors across languages so that the strengths, weaknesses, and application of the various teaching approaches under consideration would receive a more complete airing. Furthermore, there was the concomitant benefit that peer teaching sessions could be more realistic, since no single target language was shared by all members of any subgroup.

The schedule was planned so that each GTA supervisor would present some lectures to the whole group, work with the mixed language subgroups, and have time to work with his or her own GTAs to discuss issues of specific interest and to practice teaching approaches that might be particularly useful in that language or more favored in that department.

Structure of the Workshop

Each GTA supervisor took one or two turns presenting the general session lectures. Topics addressed included a shock language lesson, a film on the Dartmouth Intensive Language Model, basic concepts in language pedagogy, the psychological and emotional climate of the language classroom, teaching the first day, presenting the dialogue, teaching grammar, listening comprehension, pronunciation, reading, writing, culture, communicative competence, testing, and using the language laboratory and other media. At the end of each lecture, the presenter would usually give an assignment for the practicum-discussion sessions the following morning. Such an assignment might be to teach a dialogue in five minutes, to select a difficult phoneme in your language and teach it to the group, to present a simple grammar point (both inductive and deductive presentations had been discussed) and have the group practice using it, or to teach a mini-lesson on culture.

Often the students were required to read selections from a basic teacher training text in preparation for the lectures. Both Kenneth Chastain, *Developing Second-Language Skills: Theory to Practice* (2nd ed., Chicago: Rand McNally, 1976), and Edward D. Allen and Rebecca M. Valette, *Classroom Techniques: Foreign Languages and English as a Second Language* (New York: Harcourt, 1977), have been used.

In the afternoon each GTA supervisor met separately with his or her GTAs to allow concentration on matters of specific concern to each department: familiarization with the text(s) and materials with which the GTAs would be teaching, demonstration of, and practice with, specific teaching approaches useful for that language, preparation of texts, teaching the more advanced aspects of the language, and clarification of departmental administrative and policy guidelines.

Student Reactions to the Workshop

If students reacted differently on many points, there was unanimity on the value of the practice opportunities that the workshop made available to them. They also liked having the opportunity to become acquainted with their colleagues, with the city and the university, and with GTAs from other language departments, before the term started. They enjoyed learning a bit of one another's languages, and they liked the variety of instructors and ideas that the mixed faculty provided. In general, they commended the conception and organization of the workshop.

On the negative side, there was a definite feeling that the workshop had been too long, too strenuous, too intensive. (Interestingly, however, over two-thirds of the students who completed the course evaluation form could name no topic that should be cut down or deleted.) The students were not particularly enthusiastic about the lecture portion of the workshop or with the readings, which supports the finding that what they liked most of all was the opportunity to do practical work.

Faculty Reactions to the Workshop

Each faculty member was asked to write a short summary of his or her reactions to the workshop. Features of the workshop that received favorable mention included the cooperative spirit shown by the faculty, and the same cooperativeness shown during the following term's teaching by the GTAs; the supervisors' having more time to spend on substantive matters of teaching and testing, rather than on basic skills, when meeting during the quarter with the supervisees; the quality of teaching done by the GTAs as reflected in their classroom presence, the soundness of their lesson planning, and their mastery of basic teaching skills; and the GTAs' palpable sense of the worth of the common venture and their feeling of collegiality with the other teaching members of the department.

The faculty members also had several criticisms and suggestions for improving the workshop: the workshop was too long and too strenuous for GTAs and faculty alike; the mixed-language sessions needed better coordination; the quality of the lectures was uneven; the inapplicability of some topics covered in the lectures to GTAs in classical languages had to be resolved; the de facto extension of the fall term for faculty involved in the course must be dealt with.

Administration and Functioning of the Workshop

Admission. The requirements for admission to, and attendance at, the workshop are set by each department and are sent by the departments to their incoming GTAs, along with the letter offering support, during the preceding spring. In general, participation is mandatory for all new GTAs (though most GTA supervisors indicate that exceptions might be made for GTAs with significant experience and training in the teaching of foreign languages); the only prerequisite is acceptance as a GTA.

Credit and grading. The amount of credit awarded, the standards for grading, whether to award grades as opposed to satisfactory/unsatisfactory marks, and whether the credit received counts toward the graduate degree are all matters left up to the individual departments.

The jurisdictional question of a College of Humanities granting credit for a workshop whose focus is plainly pedagogical was resolved by an agreement between several language departments and the College of Education to cross-list the course and to maintain a consultative relationship with that college's faculty in foreign language education. This accommodation was facilitated because several of the language departments' GTA supervisors hold doctorates in foreign language education or have other professional education background and because the departments share a sincere commitment to provide training that the College of Education could not offer.

Funding. GTA stipends for the regular quarter's work are paid from a college-wide budget that is not related to departmental operating funds. The additional money needed to pay GTAs who attended the course (the amount equaled an additional one-sixth of what GTAs receive for the normal twelve-week quarter) also came from this budget. Faculty received no supplementary compensation, although in most departments some reduction in teaching load for the ensuing year was made. Course costs were offset by the increased state subsidies received by the university as a result of the graduate credit hours the course generated.

In-Service Supervision of GTAs

Whereas considerable coordination among departments in offering the workshop has been achieved, ongoing supervision during the GTAs' ensuing teaching is still entirely a departmental matter. In most departments, the supervision of new in-service GTAs is treated as a continuation of the course into the fall quarter; then it takes the form of an ongoing, no-credit activity for succeeding terms. One department, Slavic, makes a distinction between the preterm course work and the supervised teaching. This system is described below.

Most departments' in-service programs have the following: the GTA supervisor, perhaps assisted by other members of the department, makes two or three visits to a GTA's class during the first quarter of the GTA's teaching and continues to make two or three visits per quarter during the rest of the year. The supervisor meets with the GTA following each visit and discusses the class; a written record of the visit and of the discussion may or may not be made, depending on departmental procedures. The supervisor also meets weekly or biweekly with all the GTAs under his or her supervision to discuss and coordinate their actual teaching. In some instances the supervisor also assigns additional readings and provides supplementary formal instruction on teaching methods. Almost all departments require that their GTAs observe other teachers; this requirement may mean observation of a demonstration section taught by an experienced GTA or a faculty member, or it may take the form of required visits among GTAs, not necessarily within the same department. Some departments give tests and require papers of their GTAs during this first quarter of supervised teaching; others do not.

The Training Program in Slavic: A Specific Example

No single departmental training program can be said to be "typical" or "representative" of the others. Nevertheless, some specific examples taken from the Slavic program might be of interest.

The preservice course in Slavic earns the GTA three units of graded graduate credit that count toward the graduate degree. The requirements for the preservice component are:

> Participating in the common core morning program of lectures, readings, and peer teaching.
> Participating in the language-specific afternoon program. This program covers consideration of the specific materials used in the elementary Russian sequence, departmental policies and procedures, the language laboratory's role in the elementary Russian sequence, specific ways to approach the teaching of certain grammar points, preparing and using visual aids, and other matters.
> Completing an assigned project, such as preparing a set of visual aids, a series of lesson plans for a specific chapter, a set of listening comprehension exercises, or a test over specific material.
> Passing an examination over the content of the general session lectures and readings.
> Reporting on five classroom visits done during the fall quarter following the preterm workshop. These reports are written so as not to identify the instructor who was visited.

The Slavic Department is unique in that the in-service, or "supervised teaching," component of the training program is handled separately from the preservice component. For the in-service component the GTA in Slavic registers for two units of individual studies work each quarter during his or her first three quarters of teaching. Only satisfactory/unsatisfactory marks are awarded for this in-service component. The GTA's responsibilities during this phase of the program include:

Teach an assigned classroom section of elementary or intermediate Russian.

Meet one hour weekly with the GTA supervisor and the other GTAs teaching the same level courses to discuss teaching techniques for specific lessons, prepare and coordinate examinations, and clarify grading and administrative policies as needed.

Videotape one of his or her classes, view the tape privately or with the supervisor (the choice is the GTA's), and submit a written self-critique.

Meet individually with the GTA supervisor after each of the supervisor's visits to the GTA's class to discuss the lesson (there are two or three visits per quarter). After each such visit and meeting the GTA supervisor writes a letter to the GTA, making a record of the visit and summarizing the content of the discussion. A copy of the letter is forwarded to the department chairman to be placed in the GTA's department file.

Responsibilities of Beginning GTAs

Generally speaking, GTAs teach the beginning language sequence. A typical teaching load is one course that meets five times per week during the quarter. More experienced GTAs may teach second-year courses, depending on departmental policies and needs. Each department has, of course, a standard text and syllabus; the syllabus may be quite general or quite detailed regarding weekly or even daily lesson planning. Some departments allow GTAs individually to prepare and grade all the examinations for their classes; others coordinate the preparation and grading of only the final examination; others coordinate the preparation and grading of all tests. All departments make the formal statement that satisfactory teaching and satisfactory progress toward the degree are conditions for reappointment. Graduate student representatives—not necessarily GTAs—attend faculty meetings and may be appointed to various departmental committees as well. To date there have been no serious grievance actions among GTAs in the foreign language departments.

Prospects for the Future and Issues in Need of Resolution

The current interdepartmental effort will doubtless continue. It has received support at all levels: from the Dean of the College of Humanities, from department chairpersons, from faculty members (both those engaged in the training and supervision of GTAs as well as those who are not directly involved), and from the GTAs themselves.

To be sure, some areas still need attention. Among them:

Standardization across departments in credits awarded for the course, for supervised teaching, and in grading and testing policies, will probably be sought.

The matter of faculty compensation for the extra two weeks of full-day preterm teaching needs to be resolved.

The schedule of the workshop must be examined to determine whether it is, in fact, too ambitious for the time allotted and, if so, where adjustments can be made.

The curriculum needs to be reexamined in order to establish an improved balance between the theoretical and the practical aspects of the workshop.

While for the most part GTAs in both the modern and classical languages found the workshop worthwhile, in some instances topics of concern to one group were not of direct interest to the other. The scheduling of these

topics needs to be reviewed so that no group feels its time is being wasted.
A significant proportion of elementary language instruction at Ohio State
University occurs in a separate individualized instruction program. Consideration should be given to the need for training and supervising GTAs
who will be assigned not to a classroom but rather to the individualized
instruction centers.

Summary and Conclusion

For the language departments at Ohio State University, arriving at the present
status in the apprentice program for GTAs has been an evolutionary process—
one that is certainly not yet complete and likely never will be. New developments and emphases in foreign language teaching methodology, the benefits of
sharing information and procedures with other departments and other colleges,
the changing needs of GTAs and their students, and changing administrative
policies all will have an effect on the future of this program. It can be safely
said, however, that a firm foundation in the training and education of apprentice foreign language teachers has been established, and the results have more
than justified the resources invested.

Note

¹ The author wishes to recognize Professors David P. Benseler and Leon Twarog for
the conception and initiation of this program; Professors Thérèse Bonin, Mario Iglesias,
Mark Morford, and Heimtraut Taylor for their assistance in coordinating and teaching
in the program; and Dean Diether Haenicke, Assistant Dean E. Garrison Walters (both of
the College of Humanities), and the chairpersons of the foreign language departments for
their continuing support of the program.

University of Oregon, Department of English

Kathleen E. Dubs

The Department of English has had a teaching apprentice program for many
years. It began on a small scale, with the few graduate students involved
serving as assistants to regular members of the faculty who were teaching
writing. As the number of graduate students grew, the number of regular
faculty who were teaching writing proved insufficient to staff the program, and
graduate students who wanted to apprentice were assigned to work with experienced graduate students who filled the same role as the members of the
regular teaching staff. Gradually, Directors of the Composition Program came
to feel that in addition to the practical experience graduate students were
getting in the apprentice program they needed some sort of theoretical background, and so instituted the composition seminars. Originally at these
seminars graduate students gathered once a week (often at the director's
home) to present and discuss reports on theoretical or pedagogical materials.
This program further expanded, and in recent years prospective graduate
teaching fellows at the university have been required to undertake two terms
of this composition workshop—no longer a seminar, it is a workshop or, as
some have said, a sweatshop—not only to become aware of different theories of

the teaching of writing but to discuss in more pragmatic terms actual problems that come up in writing classes. Thus the current program is one that has evolved over the past ten years to its present state.

The objectives and purposes of the program generally are to train individuals to teach writing at the university level and, specifically, to teach writing at this university, where two terms of writing are an academic requirement for graduation. Further, the apprentice program and the workshops are designed to instill in the potential teacher an understanding of what teaching involves and the kind of commitment it takes—in terms of emotion, time, and intellectual effort; to offer the opportunity to learn to balance both a teaching and a scholarly career—because, after all, graduate students attend classes while they are teaching; to provide specific practical as well as theoretical materials that teachers can adopt, refine, and use in any way they find effective; to provide a support group of peers and mentors who can be helpful to them as long as the teaching fellows are teaching at the university and, in some instances, even after that. As a by-product of these efforts we hope that prospective teachers who do decide after this experience that teaching is something they want to do will have got adequate support to reduce their level of anxiety, as new teachers, to the point that they can actually experience the rewards and the joy, the actual fun of teaching, from the beginning. We also, obviously, feel a responsibility to the undergraduates who are required to take these courses, and we feel that even though we have a captive audience and relatively inexperienced teachers, the undergraduates should get the best education possible.

The program is organized strictly within the department; it requires no extra funding. The Director of Composition not only directs the program but actively participates in it. The workshops, for example, are conducted by the Director of Composition. The faculty who participate in this program participate as volunteers, most of the time as eager volunteers. This is, therefore, the sort of program that could be established in any department with faculty or graduate students who are already experienced in the teaching of writing, some of whom (ideally) might have a background in pedagogy, either from rhetoric, linguistics, or education.

The stage at which prospective graduate teaching fellows are eligible to enter the program depends on the individual graduate students, but we encourage them to begin during their first term. There are really no selection procedures except self-selection, assuming that there has been no prior teaching experience. For the past few years, most graduate students have come to the University of Oregon with some form of teaching experience at the high school or college level. For experienced individuals, full participation in the training program is not usually required, although it is urged and many take advantage of various aspects of the program. For those graduate students who come with no teaching experience the following program is prescribed. During the first term of the graduate students' registration at the university they enroll in English 508, Composition Workshop, for one hour of graduate credit. This preteaching workshop, which meets one evening per week for three hours, covers the subject matter and practical problems generally encountered by a teacher of freshman composition. The workshop syllabus begins with the selection of textbooks and the preparation of a syllabus (the complexity of which usually amazes graduate students) and works its way through constructing assignments, teaching individual units (points of grammar, rhetorical modes, elements of style, and so forth), conducting class discussions, using student work in class, evaluating papers, handling plagiarism, grading standards and policies, managing problems and situations that arise in the classroom ("What do I do if a student falls asleep?"), and so forth. The agenda of each workshop is announced in advance to the department, and all interested persons are invited to attend. Of late, graduate students from outside the English Department have populated the course—students in creative writing, comparative literature, interdisciplinary graduate programs, even students in education. The workshop also recommends but does not require materials (current and classic) on theoretical and pedagogical topics, many of which are available at the composition office. The substance of the workshop, however, is practical. Members of the group wrestle with the topic under study. If nothing else, they learn that there are no quick and easy solutions, no one right answer.

During the winter term prospective teachers are not required to participate in any formal training. In the spring term, however, they are paired with experienced instructors of composition—regular members of the faculty, instructors, or senior graduate teaching fellows—in an apprentice relationship that covers the full range of the teaching experience. (In our attempts to discover a unisex term for this arrangement we hit upon "sorcerer and apprentice.") Whereas the workshop gave the prospective teachers background for the course, the apprenticeship gives them actual experience in the classroom.

In pairing sorcerers and apprentices two considerations are of equal importance. The first involves the personalities of the individuals paired. It is essential to match an apprentice with an experienced instructor who teaches in a manner the apprentice can successfully imitate. Nothing can be more frustrating than having a low-keyed, structured individual working with an in-class whirlwind. We recognize the validity of both types of teaching, and of ranges in between, and try to pair individuals who will be personally as well as professionally compatible. The second consideration is the course being taught. We feel that the individual is more important than the course, but we do insist that apprentices serve in a course they will probably be teaching in the fall—which would be one of the two required freshman composition courses, usually the first. We have often assigned these courses to our best, most experienced teachers specifically so that they might undertake the role of sorcerer in the spring.

Whenever possible, before the term begins the sorcerer and the apprentice discuss the rationale involved in planning the course—often the entire structure of the course, including not only the day-to-day schedule but the goals and objectives as well as the means. These are often the most significant and difficult sessions, but the initial agreements are essential: the two must speak, with one confident voice, a rationale accepted and understood by all. Once the term begins, the apprentice attends, and participates in, class regularly, and when the dynamics of the class are right (a mystical moment known intuitively by the sorcerer, dreaded by the apprentice, and eagerly anticipated by the class) conducts class, makes assignments, evaluates papers, and confers with students. For some sorcerers-apprentices this system is modified. For those instructors who teach largely through conferences, for example, the apprentice may assume instructional responsibility for three or four students for the duration of the term, taking charge (under supervision) of the entire syllabus for this "mini-class." Others prefer to have the apprentice teach for short periods (10-15 minutes) on several occasions and work up to full class periods. Variations are perhaps as numerous as the apprentices involved. Arrangements are made with the pair and the Director of Composition to ensure that the personalties of the individuals match the work relationship and that whatever arrangement is reached the experiences of the apprentice will as fully as possible prepare the individual for the assumption of classes in the fall. The one constant is professionalism.

The Director of Composition supervises this program and whenever appropriate meets with either or both parties of each pairing to discuss progress or problems. In addition, all participating individuals meet usually three times during the term: at the beginning to establish ground rules, during the term to compare notes and to commiserate, and at the end of the term to review and evaluate the experience. (Unofficial consultation, of course, goes on all the time.) For this full-term student-teaching experience students also receive one hour of graduate credit for English 502: Supervised College Teaching. This apprenticeship program not only gives valuable teaching experience to the prospective graduate teaching fellow; it provides invaluable supervisory experience for graduate teaching fellows in the responsible work of training another teacher of composition. The Director of Composition is the ultimate supervisor of the entire program, as part of the directorship. There is no compensation for either the director or the sorcerers—other than the opportunity to make a very real contribution to the program and to the apprentice, and, of course, there is the kind of compensation we all experience as teachers. At the end of the term, the sorcerer writes an evaluation of the apprentice's performance, makes specific suggestions for continued improvement, and recommends whether or not the apprentice should be considered for an appointment. This evaluation is shared with the apprentice and discussed by the apprentice, the instructor, and the director. At this point (if not before), apprentices fully realize the work, responsibility, and rewards involved in teaching. For some this experience is exhilarating, of course, and they can hardly wait for classes of their own. For others, it is disappointing, and they decide not to continue. A few are encouraged not to continue. We feel that this is the time for such decisions on the part of the prospective teacher and the experienced supervisors.

During the first two terms—fall term workshop, winter term "lying fallow"—prospective teachers are encouraged to volunteer their time as tutors in the writing lab at the Learning Resource Center, where they can receive training in tutoring methods as well as experience in working with students in conference. Furthermore, prospective teachers are encouraged, if they desire, to register (as part of their graduate course of study) for courses or seminars pertinent to the teaching of composition. These regular graduate courses have ranged from the traditional methods courses to seminars in classical rhetorical theory, linguistics and composition, rhetoric and the teaching of writing, and so on. Although these courses are not required, many students choose one course or an entire Ph.D. specialty in the area of rhetoric and composition.

The employment status of the teaching apprentice is undefined. The apprentice is not considered an employee in that there is no financial remuneration; the apprentice does, however, receive graduate credit, which goes on the permanent record as graduate-level training in the teaching of writing. The only contractual arrangements are the tacit agreements made individually with the sorcerer, the Director of Composition, and with the program as it exists. The appointment usually lasts for one term, although on occasion apprentices have been asked to repeat the apprenticeship because of problems encountered during the initial experience. A few, as indicated, do not satisfactorily complete the apprenticeship and do not continue. Apprentices, naturally, do not wish to be reappointed as apprentices; they wish to be appointed to courses of their own. Grievance procedures are simple: apprentices (or sorcerers) bring their grievances to the Director of Composition or the Head of the Department for resolution. Depending on the nature of the grievance, it might be referred to a department committee. Apprentices participate in department affairs as graduate students, which in this department means full participation on committees and at department meetings. The apprentice teacher has no special status outside the status of graduate student in the department, but is fulfilling requirements for both a teaching fellowship and the Ph.D. (Teaching experience is required for the Ph.D.) Once the apprenticeship has been satisfactorily completed and academic progress demonstrated, after this two-term training program, if students receive classes of their own, they receive well in advance a battery of pedagogical tools for assistance: an instructor's manual, the textbook list (they choose from approximately four), suggested syllabi for each text, possible assignments, and so forth. (New graduate teaching fellows who have teaching experience and are thus not required to participate in the training program also receive this package.) In addition, whenever possible the new graduate teaching fellows continue to consult unofficially with their sorcerers, thus having someone close at hand in addition to the Director of Composition, who knows their teaching and who can offer encouragement and advice. This mentor relationship is especially helpful for new teachers who need extra attention, as well as for continuing teachers who are on probationary one-term appointments. During this first teaching term, new graduate teaching fellows once again return to the composition workshop (English 508), where they mix with prospective teachers and other new teachers like themselves, and participate as resource persons; they raise actual problems and situations that occur in their classrooms.

Winter term, which is then the second term of their actual teaching, these new teachers participate in an active program of class visitation. (Class visitation among regular, experienced staff is an ongoing process in composition.) Every new graduate teaching fellow visits every other new graduate teaching fellow (we average ten a year); then the group meets to discuss the observations in detail. These sessions—constructive, critical, commiserative—are perhaps the most useful for the new teachers, offering them the opportunity to observe various teaching styles and to receive criticisms from peers concerning their strengths and weaknesses in the classroom.

This four-term training program, extended over a period of almost two academic years, has produced a core of graduate teaching fellows and instructors whose regular term evaluations (by students) have been consistently above the average of the university and whose students feel that their writing skills have improved markedly (according to student comment as well as instructor evaluation). It has produced a group of teachers who appreciate the teaching of writing as a professional pursuit.

One major problem with a program such as this, as with any graduate student situation, is that we must deal with the "employment pool" as it comes to us. We cannot proceed as though we were recruiting, interviewing, screening, and hiring instructors. Thus we have to work with a few graduate students who still consider the teaching of writing a necessary evil that must be endured in order to support their academic work. This can pose problems for staff morale as well as for the actual quality of the teaching. Another problem involves the difficulty encountered when a graduate teaching fellow, either at the prospective teaching stage or during the actual term of teaching, proves unsatisfactory in the classroom. The need to follow union procedures is of less concern than the problem of a less than competent teacher with demonstrated scholarly ability. (Graduate teaching fellowships, unfortunately, have come to be considered rights rather than privileges, often by faculty as well as by the graduate students themselves.) But the number of individuals who pose this kind of problem is small and they can be dealt with individually, as they have been. A final problem in achieving the goals of this program is a result of its structure. Since it is highly structured—over four terms, in nearly two academic years—students who wish to enter at a point other than the beginning find themselves in a difficult situation. Since the English Department admits students at winter and spring terms, prospective teachers may be deterred from a possible appointment simply because they were not able to participate in the workshop fall term by virtue of not having been here. The same is true for the apprenticeships in the spring. Wherever possible we try to be flexible in setting up apprentice programs, but it has not been possible to conduct the workshop other than in the fall term. We try to accommodate individuals by providing as close to equivalent work as we can, one of the seminars or graduate courses referred to above, or by training students "out of sync." Individual accommodation has been possible in the past, but is not the most desirable of alternatives.

As far as future plans and prospects are concerned, expansion is one goal: to include in the workshop and the apprentice program graduate students or others who are not graduate students in English, and given the declining enrollments of English graduate students, this is a very real possibility. There is also the possibility that, should the Director of Composition be someone whose area of specialty is not linguistics or rhetoric or composition, other members of the faculty would assume portions of this program, necessitating a structural reorganization at the top.

The teacher training program as it exists works well for us: for the faculty, for the graduate students, and for the undergraduates. It has been effective in producing people who not only do a fine job of teaching in our own writing program but go on to do well as teachers of writing elsewhere. We also feel that we produce people who do well as teachers of teachers of writing elsewhere.

University of Pittsburgh, Department of General Linguistics

Mary Newton Bruder

The Department of General Linguistics has offered M.A. and Ph.D. degrees in Linguistics within the Faculty of Arts and Sciences since 1964. Those students who successfully complete the English as a Second/Foreign Language (ES/FL) electives are awarded a Certificate in Teaching English to Speakers of Other Languages (TESOL) by the department upon completion of the degree. Approximately ninty-five percent of the sixty-one students awarded an M.A. since 1974 chose to work toward the TESOL certificate. Since 1974, fifty-eight certificates have been awarded both to United States residents and to students from abroad. Students are admitted to the Linguistics Department on the basis of a minimum undergraduate average of B and strong recommendations.

For students who choose to work for the TESOL certificate, almost every aspect of the M.A. program can be seen as an element of the teacher training program. The overall goal of the program is to train professional teachers who can function effectively in virtually any ES/FL situation. The program provides thorough training in both theoretical and applied linguistics as well as pedagogical theory and practice. Teachers-in-training combine courses in theory and/or pedagogy with practical teaching experience in a carefully designed sequence from concrete to abstract and from controlled to uncontrolled as the teacher matures in his or her experience.

In order to understand how the program operates, it is necessary to outline the organizational relationship between Linguistics and the teaching area—the English Language Institute (ELI)—as well as the relationship of the academic courses to the progression of teaching experiences.

The English Language Institute offers English as a Second Language (ESL) training to high school graduates from abroad who wish to matriculate in colleges and universities in the United States, not necessarily at the University of Pittsburgh. One of the directors is Chairman of General Linguistics, the other a Lecturer in Linguistics; both teach in the Linguistics Department and design the teacher training courses as well as the curriculum for the ELI.

Previous teaching experience is not a requisite for admission to the Linguistics Department, but it is for teaching in the ELI. ELI students pay tuition and have qualified teachers, not teacher trainees, as instructors. Prospective teachers who enter the Linguistics Department without teaching experience are offered such an opportunity in conjunction with "Techniques and Procedures" so that they can qualify, at the M.A. level, for a Teaching Assistantship (TA) or, at the Ph.D. level, for a Teaching Fellowship (TF) the following term.

The sequence of the academic program has developed over the years to prepare the trainees for their teaching assignments, which are carefully chosen on the basis of the trainees' prior experience and training as well as on their progress through the program. Basically, we try to assign first-term TA/TFs to beginning ELI classes, where the curriculum is well established and a minimum of specialized linguistic knowledge is required of the teacher.

Chart A shows a common academic course sequence through the program with a TESOL certificate specialization. Probable ELI teaching assignments are shown at the right. The chart is followed by a description of the ELI course sequence in detail for teaching English to foreign students.

CHART A
Academic Program

	Linguistics	TESOL	ELI Teaching

1st term	Phonetics/Phonemics
	Grammatical Analysis
		Techniques & Procedures	Level 1
			  Grammar
			  Pronunciation
			  Writing

2nd term	Phonology
	Syntax
		Structure of English	Level 2
			  Grammar
			  Pronunciation
			  Reading (1 & 2)

3rd term	(Various)	Theory & Method (Language Laboratory)	

4th term	(Historical Linguistics)
	(History of Linguistics)
	(Sociolinguistics)
		(Teacher Supervision)	Level 3
			  Lab Classes
			  (All Skill Areas)

5th term	(Psycholinguistics)
	Comprehensive Exams:
	  Linguistics
		(Materials)
		Comprehensive Exams:
		  TESOL
			All Skill Areas

6th term	(Various) Completion of Long Paper	(Various)	All Skill Areas

A common sequence of courses leading toward an M.A. in Linguistics with a certificate in TESOL. Related ELI teaching experiences are listed on the right.

English Language Institute course structure.

Level 1 (Teaching of English as a Foreign Language [TOEFL] courses numbered up to 375) Twenty hours per week, i.e., five hours four days each week.

Grammar—Oral grammar and communicative competence.

Pronunciation—Oral skills, spelling, and communicative competence activities.

Reading—Group and individualized reading. Emphasis on amount and comprehension. Vocabulary development.

Writing—Group and individualized work. Basic sentence structure.

Laboratory—Two to three smaller classes in one. Supplements other classes.

Level 2 (TOEFL 375-450) Same arrangement as Level 1, except:

Reading—Speed, comprehension, and vocabulary building are stressed. Most activities are done as a class.

Writing—Paragraph and composition work are emphasized, also some rhetorical organization.

Level 3 (TOEFL 450-500) Academic preparation stressed in all skill area classes.

Speaking and Grammar—(2 hours daily) Oral skills such as seminar presentations, giving and taking notes on lectures, discussing, disagreeing, and so forth.

Reading—Advanced reading skills such as skimming, scanning, guessing from context, speed and comprehension of technical materials.

Writing—Research skills and advanced rhetorical patterns. Major goal is to write a (short) acceptable research paper in the students' major field.

Description of TESOL courses.

Linguistics 239—Theory and Method of Language Teaching. This course is an introduction to the various theories and methods employed in second language teaching with a special emphasis on their linguistic and psychological foundations. A critical evaluation of both traditional approaches and more recent modern innovations will be made, with the goal of providing potential language teachers with a well-grounded but eclectic theory of language pedagogy. Students will be evaluated on the basis of tests and a term paper. Readings will be drawn from both a text and articles on reserve.

Linguistics 242—Techniques and Procedures in Language Teaching. This course is designed for teachers or teacher trainees who will teach a foreign language, especially English as a foreign or second language. The course touches minimally on pedagogical theory; concentration is on actual classroom procedures and techniques. Concurrent supervised practice teaching is required of those students who are not currently teaching a foreign language.

Linguistics 243—Seminar: Adaptation and Development of Materials for Language Teaching. Designed to introduce students to the systematic design and development of materials and texts for the teaching of second languages, the course is conducted as a seminar with student presentations on the various aspects of requirements for materials designed to teach the skills of listening, speaking, reading, and writing. Students also present a project prospectus including purpose, descriptive objectives, operational objectives, concepts, and procedures for incorporating concepts into the materials. They further prepare the materials (or part of the materials, depending on the scope of the project) and present an interim report on their project.

Linguistics 290—Seminar in ESL Teacher Supervision (1 credit). Approximately fifteen hours per term of seminar discussion/videotape observation on topics such as objectives and techniques of supervision, classroom visitations, interview and feedback to teacher, and evaluation of overall teaching. Open to anyone who has taken Linguistics 242 and has taught under the supervision of the ELI or LAI.

Linguistics 291—Practicum in ESL Teacher Supervision (3 credits). Approximately forty-five hours per term consisting of the work for Linguistics 290 plus organizing the Spouses' Course and supervising the teachers, observation of selected 242 sessions and of 242 peer teaching sessions, concluding with a three-page (maximum) report on the experience. Open to students who have taken Linguistics 242 and who have had a minimum of two terms of ELI teaching. Selection will be made according to the needs of the Spouses' Course by the ELI administrative staff on the basis of teaching performance and supervisory potential.

The full-time ELI staff consists of the codirectors mentioned above, an assistant director, a student adviser, a testing supervisor, and a staff administrator. All elements of the ELI are under direct control of the administrative staff: selecting texts, establishing curricula, placing students, and so forth. In addition to specified administrative duties, each staff member oversees certain areas of the curriculum and supervises the teachers in that area.

The duties of teacher trainees in the ELI who are hired as teaching assistants or teaching fellows occupy twenty hours per week, eight devoted to classroom teaching and the rest to preparation, correction of papers, student conferences, staff meetings, and other meetings including those with class and curriculum supervisors. The teachers receive a stipend plus tuition remission for teaching the classes. Virtually all materials are provided for the teachers; we believe that teacher trainees should put their efforts into learning to teach and not into curriculum or materials development.

In addition to a general orientation to the ELI for new people, all the teachers are oriented to the specific classes they will teach by the curriculum supervisors. Books, sample lesson plans, and instruction in basic techniques are provided at the initial meeting each term. Subsequent section meetings keep supervisors aware of problems and keep the teachers updated on one another's progress and problems.

During the second and third terms of each year the staff meet in informal teaching seminars at which there are general topics for consideration, such as cross-cultural communication and problems with specific students, culture shock, grading, cheating, discipline—topics that are recycled from the methods courses through the teaching experience. The leaders are usually from the administrative staff, but the sharing among first- and second-year trainees has been invaluable. It provides an outlet for frustrations for the beginners and a leadership role for the more experienced teachers.

As the people move through the linguistics program and achieve more and more sophistication they are assigned to the less well developed areas of the curriculum to try their hands at both materials and curriculum design. These assignments are often made in conjunction with a special interest in an area of advanced academic courses.

The teacher trainees may be divided into three basic categories according to their ELI teaching and their progression through the program: (a) untrained-inexperienced, that is not qualified to teach in the ELI; (b) trained and/or experienced, qualified to teach in ELI in a controlled situation; (c) both trained and experienced, qualified to teach in "difficult" curricular areas. A fourth group of master teachers from category (c) are recommended to take the courses in teacher supervision during the second year, and these advanced students become supervisors for the category (a) students during their initial training.

In conjunction with the first-term TESOL course, Techniques and Procedures in TESOL, the neophyte teachers begin their teaching experience with classes of foreign student spouses, who pay a nominal fee for about thirty hours of English instruction per term. The classes meet on a regularly scheduled basis—about three times per week—attendance is taken, a set curriculum is followed, lessons are planned; in short, we try to replicate as much as possible conditions that will be encountered in the ELI. The teachers also have immediate opportunities for trying out ideas from the academic course.

As mentioned above, second-year "master" teachers enrolled in the seminar on supervision oversee the beginners. They help with lesson plans and observe frequently, offering feedback on all aspects of the lesson. The supervision trainees are further supervised by a permanent ELI staff member, and the seminar is run by one or both of the ELI directors, who also teach Techniques and Procedures. In this manner we try to ensure that initial teaching experience is unified and rewarding.

Linguistics students who enter the degree program with training and experience in language teaching, such as Peace Corps experience, begin to teach in the ELI in the Level 1 and 2 courses, where the curriculum is set, materials are selected, homework assignments and often tests have been previously prepared by the institute. The main task for the teacher is to run the class smoothly, correct papers, and keep the students learning. First-term students in linguistics take Techniques and Procedures; teachers whose background is weak can use this time to hone their skills and outstanding teachers can familiarize themselves with the institute.

Once the teachers have shown that they are competent and capable of managing the carefully controlled classes, they are assigned to the upper-level classes, which are more difficult because the curriculum is more flexible since student academic needs vary and less is known about teaching ESL at advanced levels, so more experimentation takes place. This is not to imply that the teachers have license to do as they wish; the texts are still chosen by the staff and the curriculum is set for a given term, but within those parameters there is a great deal of freedom.

Ideally, the student who earns our Linguistics M.A., with TESOL certificate, has made the entire progression through the categories at an incremental pace so that we may recommend him or her for virtually any ES/FL job that presents itself. But this is not always the case. Some teachers have problems with items such as academic studies, discipline, motivation, lesson planning, and so on. Clearly, these teachers are not going to progress through the sequence at the same rate as the others mentioned above.

All classes are observed at least twice each term by the curriculum supervisor for the given skill area. A common evaluation form is used throughout the institute and becomes part of the teacher's permanent record. The teacher and supervisor discuss the lesson as soon as possible after the observation.

We are implementing a review process during the third term of ELI teaching experience, when the teachers will meet with one of the directors to review progress (as detailed in the evaluations) and plan the second year teaching program and/or review the type of teaching recommendations that would be likely for teachers who are finishing the program. This review procedure will provide a formal composite feedback for the trainees at various stages of their training.

Our major area of weakness is the training of non-English-speaking teachers. Since only native speakers may teach in the ELI, the international teachers do not have the same range and variety of experience as do the English speakers. We are exploring such possibilities as teacher aides, team teaching, and increased numbers of noninstitute classes to augment the present limited opportunities.

We have no major innovations in mind for the future, but it is our hope to continue to provide the broadest training program possible in linguistics and pedagogy so that our graduates can be successful in whatever teaching situations they encounter.

University of Texas, Austin, Department of Germanic Languages

Frank E. Donahue

History

Since 1977 the Department of Germanic Languages at the University of Texas at Austin has operated a teaching apprenticeship program for all teaching assistants (TAs) that consists primarily of a mandatory three-credit graduate course in foreign language pedagogy and German applied linguistics; a second, optional, three-credit graduate course in curriculum design and materials development; and a three-to-four-semester-long in-class practicum in a lower-division German course with a regular, tenured or tenure-track faculty member.

The German apprenticeship program is the result of several developments that more or less reached a climax simultaneously. By 1974 it had become clear that the quality of teaching in lower-division courses would have to improve to stave off enrollment losses and to enable the department to continue to support as many graduate students as possible through TA stipends. There was general agreement that placing inexperienced graduate students in the classroom with no formal, pedagogical training was counterproductive and less than fair to both the TAs and their students. The faculty also recognized that possession of a degree in German, whether that degree be a B.A., M.A., or Ph.D., was no guarantee of teaching ability. As a result, a formal course in language teaching was designed, and course coordination tightened considerably. At the same time, the Texas State Legislature was investigating allegations that faculty members in the University of Texas System generally were neglecting teaching, particularly of undergraduates, in favor of research projects, that few professors were active in the instruction of freshmen and sophomores, and that TAs were largely teaching intuitively because of little or no pedagogical training. The resulting legislation regulated teaching workloads for faculty and TAs, required all new TAs to complete a teaching methods course in their first semester, and, in an effort to increase faculty participation in lower-division courses and to upgrade the quality of instruction by TAs, further stipulated that no graduate student could teach a class alone as the teacher of record until he or she had earned the M.A. or M.S. degree or the equivalent number of credit hours, normally regarded as thirty. The term "teaching assistant" was to mean that the graduate student was truly an assistant, not an independent teacher. Graduate students who had completed the M.A. *and* a teaching methods course would be eligible to teach a class alone under the general supervision of a faculty member who coordinated that course. Such graduate student teachers were to be called "assistant instructors" (AIs), were afforded some additional privileges, and earned higher stipends than TAs.

TA and AI Selection

A departmental committee on financial aid and fellowships annually assesses the credentials of candidates for advanced degrees, and, on the basis of their and the graduate adviser's recommendations, the chairman appoints TAs and AIs for the following academic year. Besides solid transcripts and strong, positive letters of recommendation, applicants for stipends must attain a minimal score of 1100 on the Graduate Record Exam. Although a graduate student may become a TA or AI at any time, most assistantships and assistant instructorships are awarded at the beginning of a graduate student's career or after the M.A. degree.

There is no formal contract between the department and the TA, but the TA does receive a description of his or her duties as terms of the appointment. The TA's signature is tantamount to acceptance of those terms and their contingent responsibilities. Teaching assistants must assume a load of at least nine graduate credits per semester and are assigned to one section of a lower-division course. Normally, new TAs begin the apprenticeship practicum in the first-semester German course and continue in subsequent semesters so that they have taught the full range of lower-division courses by the time they become AIs, at which time the pedagogical training period is over. Assistant instructors must also maintain a graduate credit load of nine hours per semester, unless working on a dissertation, and they must teach a minimum of twelve undergraduate course hours per academic year, that is, approximately three or four courses. A limited number of summer teaching stipends are awarded to graduate students primarily by seniority.

Stipends

Currently there are twenty-eight TAs and AIs in the Department of Germanic Languages, and the number of graduate students supported through teaching stipends hinges directly on the status of lower-division enrollments. The funds for the stipends come from the Dean of Liberal Arts, who in turn receives budgetary allotments from the president. New TAs receive a stipend of $3,500; second-year TAs earn $3,750. As soon as the TA becomes an AI, the training period is over and the stipend jumps to $4,500 per academic year. Assistant instructors who are writing a dissertation receive a stipend of $4,750. All TAs and AIs pay in-state tuition out of their stipends, and that amount averages approximately $250 per semester. TAs and AIs may receive financial support from the department for a maximum of ten semesters, excluding summers, as long as good progress toward the target degree continues and the quality of teaching and the participation in departmental extracurricular activities are acceptable. Only in exceptional cases has financial support been terminated.

TAs, AIs, and Departmental Governance

All graduate students, including nonteaching graduate students, have an impact on departmental decision-making in several ways, but mostly in an advisory capacity. There is a very active departmental organization of graduate students that elects its own officers to represent their views at faculty meetings, which are open to all members of the department, but at general faculty meetings only the tenured and tenure-track faculty may vote. There are a number of departmental and ad hoc committees that include graduate students as full voting members, and these committees are charged with presenting their findings at the faculty meetings. Course coordinators in the lower division actively seek the opinions and often the advice of the TAs and AIs under their supervision when formulating course policies. In general, there is a true spirit of collegial cooperation between the graduate students and the faculty, and the atmosphere has been one of progressive harmony.

Should a graduate student ever wish to file an official grievance, there is a standard, formal university policy to be followed, but no graduate student has, to anyone's memory, ever felt compelled to invoke that right. The department has, at all levels, practiced an open-door policy with regard to solving problems. The informal arrangement has been successful because of the rather open and friendly atmosphere in the department.

Goal of the Apprenticeship Training

The purpose of the program is to develop a group of teachers who will be able to function effectively and efficiently in leading our undergraduates to success in their courses and who will be able to take a leadership role in the language teaching endeavors of the departments in which they eventually find employment as faculty members. Since each graduate student possesses a unique personality, attempting to develop a corps of instructors who act and think identically is not feasible, let alone desirable. Rather than try to manufacture clones of the TA trainer in assembly-line fashion, we propose to inform the novice teachers of the options open to them, show them as many sides of pedagogical issues as possible, expose them to a broad span of methodological approaches, and give them enough elbow room to develop according to their own perceptual aptitudes, successful learning and teaching preferences, current methodological convictions, and personality traits. If we have trained them well, they will not take the path to radical extremes.

Orientation

The lower-division coordinator informs newly appointed TAs by letter, several months before their arrival on campus, about the teaching apprenticeship program and the orientation sessions prior to the beginning of the fall semester. The purpose of this letter is not only to inform but also to relieve the apprehension most new TAs confess to having during the summer months before the onset of graduate studies and teacher training. We assure these future TAs that they will not be "thrown to the lions," at least not immediately. Kenneth Chastain's *Developing Second-Language Skills: Theory to Practice* (2nd ed., Chicago: Rand McNally, 1976) is recommended for summer reading so that the new TAs might acclimate themselves to the teacher's perspective before their training.

The orientation sessions involve, besides new TAs, all the professors, instructors, assistant instructors, and "seasoned" TAs who will be teaching in the first three semester courses, and these sessions take place on two successive days the week before the semester gets underway.

Because TAs do not teach at all at the beginning of their first semester, it is not critical for them to cram all sorts of information into their heads at once. The goal of the orientation sessions is to present comprehensive information about the scope and philosophy of our language program, discuss the textual materials to be used in each course and the testing policies to be applied, and to take care of any other administrative matters at hand. In effect, the orientation sessions of the first day serve as a refresher for the experienced teachers, some of whom will not have been on campus for several months and who will not therefore be informed of any recent course revisions or modifications. Following these administrative sessions, a departmental luncheon is served so that all members of the department, new and old, will have a chance to get to know one another informally before the beginning of the semester.

The second day of orientation begins with a synopsis of the information presented previously and continues with several hours of demonstration teaching by the teaching assistants who had begun training one year earlier. We try to concretize the information and also demonstrate to the TAs the extent to which they can expect to progress pedagogically in one year. Coordination meetings for the specific lower-division courses are normally held later that day, and a tour of the language lab and media facilities caps off the orientation.

Practicum

New TAs are inserted very gradually into the teaching process. During the first three weeks, when the first chapter of the textbook, *Modern German* (ed. Van Horn Vail and Kimberly Sparks, 2nd ed. [New York: Harcourt, 1978]), is treated, the new TAs observe all teachers and all sections of the first semester course. They are expected to spend eight hours a week in class observations, and three of those hours are in the class taught by the lower-division coordinator to ensure that they see the course taught as envisioned. At the end of the observation period the TAs should have noticed that a variety of teaching styles can be effective and can prepare students rather uniformly for the next course in the lower-division sequence. They should also have profited from the many postobservation conferences held with the instructors they had visited.

It is clearly advantageous not to burden new TAs with the normal responsibilities of a teacher too early. Enough time is afforded them to adjust to the role of the teacher-student and to familiarize themselves more fully with the layout of the campus and with the departmental workings. By the time the observation period ends the TAs are usually quite eager to get their feet wet and try some teaching. They exhibit few signs of apprehension because they have been prepared mentally to stand before a class and lead it.

A key ingredient in the rest of the first semester practicum is the one-to-one ratio of TA to professor. Each TA indicates his or her preference for the faculty member with whom he or she wishes to complete the semester. We feel it is critical that the TA-professor team be as compatible personally and pedagogically as possible, and we grant as many requests as we can.

Once the TA begins classroom teaching, the satellite duties of office hours, tutorial assistance, involvement in the extracurricular functions of the department, and coordination meetings begin. The twenty hours of teaching-related work required of TAs by the State of Texas are justified as follows:

Classroom instruction	5 hours
Class preparation/homework and testing correction	10 hours

Office hours	2 hours
Tutorial assistance	1 hour
Test design and critique	1 hour
Undergraduate German Club	1 hour

During Chapter ii of the textbook the professor presents and drills all new material and the TA reviews and drills any review matter. For the duration of Chapter iii the roles are reversed, with the TA presenting and drilling the new material and the professor treating the review activities. At all phases of the practicum the TA has an opportunity to see how the professor treats a problem or task before he or she needs to repeat the same or a similar one. It also allows the TA to get a better feel for how the professor would prefer to have the class conducted, because, even though the two are working together as a team, the professor is the teacher of record for the class and is, then, the manager of the team. All parties in the apprenticeship receive clear guidelines to follow to ensure that the TA is neither over- nor underworked. The same procedure is followed in the TA's subsequent apprenticeship semesters.

An important element in the success of the apprenticeship and its positive impact on lower-division courses is this author's *Lower Division German Supplement* (Minneapolis: Burgess, 1979), a unique three-hundred-page manual used by all teachers and students in the first three semester courses. This manual contains all the theory behind the program in the form of detailed syllabi, close to a dozen study guides that address the problems in second language learning by adults and to the specific performance objectives of our lower-division course components, for example, grammar theory and drill, vocabulary acquisition, reading for comprehension, intensive reading for mastery of content and as a basis for developing oral communicative competence, test preparation through practice exams, and the integration of culture into the courses. Day-by-day class assignments for the first three semester courses ensure that students will be paced evenly through the courses—a fundamental element of overall program health—and all the textbooks are coordinated to form a tightly integrated, homogeneous program that avoids the "third semester seam" that plagues many college-level language programs. Although both the lower-division program and the apprenticeship are highly organized, they are not suffocating to the TAs or the undergraduates. There is enough room for the teachers to add their own creative stamp and for the students to engage in spontaneous language exchanges.

We recognize that the TAs are at the university primarily to pursue advanced studies, not to spend most of their time scampering here and there trying to do oftentimes painstaking busywork that robs critically needed time and energy for class preparations and graduate study. Curriculum design, development, reform, and materials production are tasks for the coordinators, not the beginning teachers, unless, of course, they wish to do these things or assist in those undertakings.

Coordination bulletins appear regularly to keep teachers both informed and poised about the peculiarities of instruction during certain phases of each course. Teaching workshops are conducted as needed or desired to focus on areas where instruction has been either inadequate or unsatisfactory. New TAs and first-time instructors in the courses are required to attend these workshop sessions. All other personnel are invited to come as they wish. These sessions, involving discussions, microteaching, and some materials generation, are scheduled at a time convenient to most, and last for approximately one hour.

Theoretical Training

We offer our graduate students a solid three-credit graduate course in foreign language pedagogy, the teaching of German, and teacher and student behavior and expose them to a broad spectrum of theoretical topics so that they may teach and grow professionally in an enlightened manner; we expect them to establish a critical stance toward language teaching just as they do in their study of German literature and philology.

All activities in the course focus primarily on college-level language teaching, although other levels of language teaching and language acquisition are examined by necessity.

In the first phase of the course the students discuss practical information regarding what to expect and demand realistically from students, how to prepare thoroughly and effectively for class, how to create an educationally fertile atmosphere in the classroom, time management inside and outside of the class, general guidelines and considerations for foreign language teachers, general principles for effective learning and teaching, and what we think we know about the successful language learner and the successful language teacher. Some elementary training in German articulatory phonetics is offered to enable the TAs to deal effectively with the pronunciation and intonation problems that characteristically confront American students.

During the second phase of the course the TAs examine the major foreign language teaching methodologies that have gained a following in this country, such as the grammar-translation, direct, audio-lingual, Berlitz, audiovisual, and cognitive methods as well as the audio-motor unit as practiced by Gouin and Asher. The students familiarize themselves with the linguistic and psychological underpinnings of each method along with the appropriate techniques and stages of instruction peculiar to each approach. Each method is assessed for strengths and weaknesses, real or potential, and for realistic chances for success with college-age students. In addition, each method is analyzed with respect to the development of the four skills and vocabulary acquisition, and the students try to determine which skills can be developed optimally with which methodological techniques. TAs are expected to experiment in their apprenticeship teaching with the techniques encountered in the methods course as part of this determination.

Other, less methodologically oriented topics, such as motivation, the teaching of culture, and the employment of various teaching aids, particularly visual media, are treated during the final phase of the course.

Throughout the course the students read in the more commonly used teacher handbooks, acquaint themselves with the more prominent foreign language and German pedagogical journals through a bibliography project, learn to use videotape cameras and playback units, and carry out a minor research project or design a set of materials for use in the class in which they are apprenticing. Of course, there is a good deal of microteaching and practice in techniques all throughout the course. Two essay exams are administered during the course, and at the end of the course each TA must be able to formulate his or her teaching philosophy in some detail and in terms that indicate the student has some control over the pedagogical jargon currently in vogue.

If enough students desire, a second course in foreign language pedagogy can be offered. This second course deals primarily with training for the kinds of tasks normally assigned to junior faculty members in larger departments: designing and supervising undergraduate courses and programs, selecting textbooks, finding sources for gathering realia, testing options, creating cultural units for in-class instruction as well as for self-study, designing visual aids, using the camera, particularly the 35mm SLR type, as a tool, and organizing extracurricular activities to complement language courses. Several projects are assigned for these areas, the major one being the development of a first-semester course and the production of such items as syllabi, daily lesson assignments for each day of the semester, study guides, and sample tests. By the end of the second course the TA should be able to exert a leadership role in lower division study and should be of real assistance with the next generation of TAs.

Evaluation of Teaching

TAs and AIs are evaluated several ways throughout their teaching careers at the University of Texas. During the first semester of graduate study, when the TA observes other teachers, he or she makes a number of recordings on audio tape for an evaluation of pronunciation and intonation. Any TA needing remedial work can consult with several faculty members who have training in applied linguistics. Should a TA need remedial work in conversational German or stylistics, he or she can audit a number of upper-level undergraduate courses for self-improvement.

Pedagogical observations of the TA are carried out principally by two faculty members, the lower-division coordinator and the practicum professor. The in-class supervising professor offers daily feedback to the TA, and the lower-division coordinator makes a minimum of three observations of the TA during the latter half of the semester and confers privately with the TA. Both professors complete a detailed evaluation of the TA's progress to date and review their evaluations with the TA. Shortly thereafter a performance plan for the next semester is drawn up so that the TA will be able to focus on an area or two that can stand improvement. A summary evaluation of the pedagogical progress of our teaching graduate students is made when the TA or AI seeks employment, and it may become part of his or her dossier.

As long as the TA continues to make satisfactory progress in teaching, he or she continues the apprenticeship in the next sequential lower-division course. If the TA might profit more from repeating an apprenticeship in the same course, he or she does so, but this time under the practicum supervision of another, different professor, who exhibits the kind of teaching behavior the TA should emulate. Every effort is made to convince the TA that such a decision is not a demotion or an indication that he or she is on the "taxi squad." We simply realize that not everyone makes pedagogical progress at the same rate, and we feel we should take a firm lead in the careful guidance and growth of each instructor. Those TAs who have repeated an apprenticeship have demonstrated clearly, to us and to themselves, that such decisions have truly been in their own best interests, and they are demonstrably better teachers as a result.

Teaching assistants working in pairs receive training in the use of videotape recording equipment from the University of Texas Center for Teaching Effectiveness, and they tape each other's classes. Having another teacher, however limited in teaching experience, do the taping is usually superior in terms of perception than taping performed by a visual laboratory technician. The TA thinks like a teacher during the videotaping; the lab technician does not. The TA has a better intuitive sense of what to shoot. Each TA evaluates his or her own tape and discusses the self-evaluation with the practicum professor and the lower-division coordinator. Normally, the TA is an accurate and tough critic, sometimes overly critical.

The undergraduate students also evaluate the TA in writing, and their criticism is usually somewhat milder and less direct than that offered by the faculty members, but their criticisms and those furnished by the professors usually reinforce what the TA has viewed on tape.

Coordinators

The faculty member who designed the lower-division program and the apprenticeship teacher training approach coordinates lower-division German. The coordinator works closely with the faculty members who serve as course coordinators to ensure that the lower-division courses flow smoothly and successfully as planned. A total of five faculty members are involved in course and program supervision, and each earns credit for supervision that is applicable toward fulfilling the state-mandated faculty workload. Each professor must amass a minimum of nine work units per semester, with one unit equal to one hour of undergraduate teaching. Coordinators earn one workload credit for every six class sections under their management, with a ceiling of three credits for supervision per semester.

Course coordinators hold coordination meetings with their teachers as needed, delegate authority for the completion of common goals, for example, test generation, observe teachers in the classroom, and function as arbiters when the need arises. Since course goals, policies, and syllabi have been worked into a comprehensive plan contained in the aforementioned *Lower Division German Supplement* and since both lower division and the teacher training programs have benefited from three years of tinkering and refinements, the administrative workload of the course coordinators has been reduced drastically. Because stability is a critical aspect of the health of any large program or comprehensive, long-range effort, coordinators are expected to commit themselves to the courses they teach and supervise and to the program of which they are a part and not try to get by on minimal effort. To date, both program and coordinator stability and consistency have been excellent and productive.

Current Assessment

Generally speaking, both the lower-division German program and the teaching apprenticeship program have been functioning like a well-oiled machine. The first-year courses in lower division have been "debugged," and the third- and fourth-semester courses are in the final refinement stages. Enrollment increases, that is, increases in retention, in the third and fourth semesters have been fifty-six percent and thirty-two percent respectively, a clear indication that our beginning German courses offer solid instruction and that our sophomore-level courses continue to hold students' interest. Enrollment gains in junior courses, that is, entry-level upper-division courses, have run as high as seventy-seven percent in at least two cases in 1980, which is another clear indicator that lower-division German is alive and well in Texas.

There have been no serious problems in the apprenticeship program to date, either in its administration or in its impact on lower-division instruction. The TAs and AIs generally have a fine grasp of the course and program goals, and most have developed a successful strategy of language teaching and a stockpile of techniques to the point where they require little over-the-shoulder supervision. They can really be counted on to function positively and professionally. The only gnawing instructional concern centers on the ability of the TAs to engage the students more in communicative tasks and in increasing the amount and quality of student oral German. The teachers who are very successful with this most challenging aspect of language teaching are those who are precise, methodical, dynamic, and innovative; in short, those who are creative and disciplined. This creative, disciplined dynamism tends more to be a function of the teacher's personality and less a methodological variable. It is, therefore, difficult to "teach" to TAs. This controlled creativity is the difference between the *Mechaniker* and the *Künstler*.

A concern that recurs from time to time is the universal problem of apathy, particularly toward the end of a semester, when fatigue begins to show. Teachers sometimes fail to perform as expected, particularly administratively, and special efforts must be made to keep the *Zusammenarbeit zusammen*. At such times the coordinators have to bear down on their colleagues a bit, a distasteful but necessary reaction.

The area of faculty support in the apprenticeship venture has been a nice surprise. Since most of the tenured faculty are graduates of the "sink or swim" school of teacher training, some apprentice TAs have a better grasp of language teaching theory and a clearer insight into the design and thinking behind the lower-division program and courses than some practicum professors. The result is more often not conflict but a sharing of the wealth: the TAs make the professor reevaluate his or her teaching philosophy, and the teacher offers and demonstrates his or her experientially acquired knowledge. Obviously, there is a potential source of conflict here, but because the TAs select their practicum professor after considerable observation time, conflict has not materialized.

Future Plans

There are no plans to change either the teaching apprenticeship system or the lower-division program, a predominantly cognitive-eclectic, four-skills program. The teaching methods course will be modified to allow for more micro-teaching than has been done previously. I am in the process of writing a book for TAs in foreign language teaching that will address their needs directly, and this volume will be the main source of theoretical reading.

There is, at the moment, a proposal before the faculty that we allow a

Ph.D. candidate to specialize in the area of foreign language teaching, German applied linguistics, teacher training, and program management. There is a clear professional need for methodologists trained within the language department who will possess the necessary linguistic skills, pedagogical expertise, and administrative abilities to direct the departmental teacher training and language programs of a university department. For too long many departments have taken those areas for granted and have placed inexperienced persons, often junior faculty, in supervisory positions for which they lack the training, and this practice must be considered one of several factors that have contributed to the decline in language study at the college level in the past decade. The faculty of the Department of Germanic Languages at the University of Texas at Austin understands fully the relationship between the health of the lower division and the number of TAs and AIs the department can support, a relationship that ultimately dictates the kinds and number of graduate courses that can be offered, which, in turn, determines whether the graduate program flourishes, stagnates, or withers.

If TA training and its impact on all levels of a university department are to be taken seriously by the profession, then so must the training of the next generation of TA trainers—and it must be taken seriously now. The prospects for adopting the proposal seem good, for we have the personnel and facilities, and the timing is right.

University of Wisconsin, Madison, Department of French and Italian

Constance K. Knop

History and Goals

The training of teaching assistants has long been considered an important task in the Department of French and Italian at the University of Wisconsin, Madison because of the large number of beginning-level courses taught by TAs and because of the basic autonomy that TAs have in their own section of a given course. In the 1950s and early 1960s, teaching assistants received training from the chairperson of the course in which they were teaching. TAs met weekly with that person to discuss points of grammar, to rework the syllabus, and to plan examinations. In addition, they were encouraged to visit demonstration classes taught by experienced TAs or faculty members. Supervision consisted primarily of a classroom visit from the course chairperson and another professor.

In 1966, in response to requests by the TAs for more extensive preparation for teaching, a one-credit, graduate-level course, College Teaching of French, was established. The course was composed of required readings, discussions, and observations of classes. In 1970 that course was expanded to a three-credit, graduate-level methods course and was made a requirement for the master's or Ph.D. degree. TAs in the course now meet for two hours a week to discuss general problems in teaching a second language, specific problems encountered in their teaching, and development of language skills. The goals of the course are to prepare TAs to teach the course to which they are assigned and to help them understand the general learning needs and problems of beginning language students. TAs visit one another's classes, view a variety of videotapes dealing with different types of lessons, write up lesson plans focusing on the development of specific skills, and analyze and evaluate a videotape of one of their own classes. For the third credit of the course, TAs meet weekly with their course chairperson to raise problems encountered in the textbook or syllabus, to prepare quizzes and examinations, and to share teaching materials. Thus, the program attempts to prepare TAs to plan effective instructional strategies and activities in a beginning language course, to understand their students' needs and problems, to develop valid tests, and to evaluate and improve their own teaching.

Organization

The Dean of the College of Letters and Sciences approves a yearly budget for hiring teaching assistants to teach courses in the first four semesters of French and Italian. The instructor of College Teaching of French has a quarter-time appointment in the department and a three-quarter-time appointment in the School of Education. Faculty members who chair one of the courses and supervise TAs in that course receive released time from other teaching responsibilities. These faculty members generally teach a section of the course that they coordinate. Other faculty members help supervise TAs on request from chairpersons of the first four levels of French.

Appointment of TAs

TAs may be appointed at any stage in their graduate studies. Most of them begin teaching in their first semester of graduate work. All new teaching assistants are required to take the methods course. Usually all new TAs are assigned to teach first-semester French. This seems to ensure more success in meeting the needs of TAs in their methods training and in supervision. Discussion in the methods course has proved more meaningful and helpful now that the TAs are all involved in the same level of teaching and are all working with similar materials. Procedures for selecting TAs include evaluation of their undergraduate work, an oral interview in French with a faculty member (a native speaker who teaches the phonetics course), and letters of recommendation.

The TAs have a union (the TAA, Teaching Assistants' Association) that bargains a contract with university officials. This contract specifies conditions for reappointment and dismissal, class size, salary, number of working hours, grievance procedures, and so forth. Although not all TAs choose to belong to the union, they are protected by the contract and services afforded by the union. Representatives from the TAA are allowed to attend open faculty meetings and to participate in discussions. They are also asked to help evaluate candidates for faculty positions that become open in the department.

Reappointment of a TA (in accordance with conditions of the contract) is determined by classroom visits from the methods professor, course chairperson, and other faculty members and also by their students' evaluations (which are completed in class at the end of the semester and handed in to the office by one of the students).

Aspects of the Training Program

The training program consists of an orientation session, a methods course taken concurrently with the first semester of teaching, meetings with course chairpersons, and continuing supervision.

Orientation session. A three-day orientation program is set up during registration week to help the TAs understand the administrative framework of the department, their roles and responsibilities, and the goals of the course to which they are assigned. In addition, training is planned to help the novice teachers understand and analyze causes of students' errors. A "shock lesson," in which the TAs learn a dialogue in Hungarian, helps sensitize them to the anxieties and needs that beginning language students are likely to experience. Alternative strategies for correcting errors are also discussed. The methods instructor demonstrates techniques for teaching grammar and pattern practices as well as basic strategies for drilling a dialogue. Videotaped segments of actual classes are also studied to reinforce the techniques demonstrated. On their own, TAs map out a first-day lesson plan and then view and analyze a tape of an actual first-day class to compare it with their own plan, to uncover alternative activities and techniques, and to prepare themselves for the types of problems that students usually have on the first day. To complete the orientation training, TAs then teach segments of their plan to one another and so gain some actual teaching experience before the first day's class.

In 1978, a survey was sent out to seventy former and present TAs in the University of Wisconsin, Madison's French Department.[1] The twenty-nine respondents (41% of the sample) evaluated aspects of their orientation session, of the methods course, and of their supervision. The following items were rank-ordered by the group as the five most useful aspects of the orientation program:

> Presentation of techniques for teaching pattern practices and teaching grammar.
> Discussion of a first-day lesson plan.
> Meetings with course chairperson.
> Teaching parts of a first-day lesson plan in the TA group.
> Introductory session on organization of the department and on roles and responsibilities of a teaching assistant.

These rankings appear to represent basic concerns that one might anticipate in beginning TAs, namely: (1) a need for clarification of their duties as a TA in a given course and within the department, (2) uncertainty and uneasiness about how to handle the first class session, and (3) a desire to master basic techniques for teaching grammar and vocabulary. Should we ever have to reduce the scope of the orientation program, we have guidelines for selecting aspects of it that TAs have found most beneficial.

Methods course. During their first semester of teaching the TAs take College Teaching of French. Textbooks for the course include: a theoretically based book (Wilga Rivers, *A Practical Guide to the Teaching of French* [New York:

Oxford Univ. Press, 1975]), a pragmatically oriented book (Edward D. Allen and Rebecca M. Valette, *Classroom Techniques: Foreign Languages and English as a Second Language* [New York: Harcourt, 1977]), a book on testing (Rebecca M. Valette, *Modern Language Testing*, 2nd ed. [New York: Harcourt, 1977]), and extensive handouts that demonstrate techniques and activities for developing various skills in a language.

In the course's two-hour session, the first part of the class is usually devoted to discussing immediate needs and concerns, such as discipline problems with students, planning more effective warm-ups, reducing "teacher talk" in the class, involving and motivating students, and so on. The TAs value this free time for releasing emotional tensions and for exchanging ideas on solving these common problems.

Readings and videotapes demonstrating aspects of a given topic are assigned each week on the syllabus. The rest of the class session deals with discussion, analysis, and application of that week's topic to one's teaching. Additional videotapes and demonstrations by the methods professor are usually included to offer concrete models to the novice teacher.

In the 1978 survey TAs were asked to assess the value and importance for teacher preparation of the topics covered in the methods course.

It is interesting to note that all the topics from the course were rated in the "moderately important/useful" category. In fact, half of them were considered in the "extremely" to "very" important/useful level. These top items deal, for the most part, with the development of the four basic skills (listening, speaking, reading, writing), with teaching pattern practices and grammar, with techniques for conducting class activities and for dealing with errors, and with making up and grading examinations. Since these topics are all a part of the day-to-day routine of teaching language in a beginning class, it is not surprising that they are highly valued by the teaching assistants. Moreover, most of these areas are also needed in teaching language at a succeeding level and so could be reused, adapting them to the continuing linguistic needs of the students. Theoretical considerations, as well as practical techniques, are included in the most highly rated topics. This would tend to reinforce the importance of blending research and theory with practical applications and demonstrated techniques in a methods course.

Working with the course chairperson. As mentioned previously, most of the beginning teaching assistants are assigned to first-semester French. Experienced TAs may be asked to teach any one of the first four semesters of French. All TAs are given guidance and help by their course chairperson, who plans a syllabus that outlines the parts of the texts that are to be covered each week. Language laboratory assignments, quizzes, and examinations are also indicated on the syllabus. The chairperson and the TAs in the course make up examinations to be administered at the fifth, tenth, and final week of classes. In this way, homogeneity of progress and achievements of all students, regardless of the individual section to which they are assigned, is ensured. TAs are responsible for making daily lesson plans, worksheets, and weekly quizzes on their own, but they are also responsible for covering the material in the text in such a fashion and in sufficient amount so that their students succeed on the departmental examinations.

In addition to planning the syllabus and training TAs in making up examinations, the chairperson develops resource files that TAs may draw on when teaching that course. This file consists of past worksheets written by other TAs to supplement the text, sample quizzes and examinations, visual aids, and cultural units. Chairpersons also set up audiovisual materials to be used in the language laboratory. These materials range from slides to films to taped interviews with native speakers. Generally, scripts accompany the materials. In this way, students may work with the materials individually, or the TAs may go over the scripts in class before assigning the materials to students.

Thus, the chairperson of the course serves as an organizer of the content of the course, as a guide in developing examination and lesson plans, and as a resource person for supplementary learning materials. Since most chairpersons teach a section of the course, they also serve as model teachers whom the TAs can visit any time during the semester for continuing training.

Supervision. Supervision is considered a crucial element in the training program. The prevailing attitude toward supervision of TAs is that the activity should be diagnostic and helpful in nature, not just evaluative. To that end, a modified version of clinical supervision is used. The four phases of a supervisory act, as outlined in clinical supervision,[2] include:

Preobservation conference. In this phase, the TA and supervisor spend 5–10 minutes discussing the lesson plan, goals for the class to be observed, and information about the group (e.g., kinds of interactions typical of them, special problems with that group). In addition, the TA usually suggests one or two areas of special concern for improvement (e.g., clarity of directions, rewards, "fading the cue," amount of teacher talk to student talk, etc.). The supervisor and TA decide on special areas or specific problems/questions to discuss after the observation, based on the TA's area(s) of concern.

Data-gathering phase. While observing the class, the supervisor takes extensive notes—verbatim if possible—on what goes on during the class hour, including teacher talk, types of student responses, physical behavior of students and teacher (e.g., teacher's movement around the class, nonverbals, students' doing other work, etc.). Judgmental comments are not usually included, except to note items to praise. Rather, objective data are accumulated for analysis and discussion later on.

TAs are encouraged not to be intimidated or depressed by the supervisor's extensive writing, as it is necessary to assemble as much information as possible for the follow-up conference.

Analysis of the data. The data are given to the TA to study, analyze, and make suggestions on. The main goals of clinical supervision are discovering recurring patterns of teacher behavior and evaluating them, discarding those found ineffective and continuing those that seem successful. Thus, in analyzing the data, the TA and supervisor should be looking for such patterns. In addition, data should be looked for that respond to the expressed concerns of the TA. If clarity of directions had been noted, then directions should be carefully studied, with alternative examples to be suggested.

It usually is a good idea to make a carbon copy of the data while observing. In this way, both the supervisor and TA have a chance to examine the data and make analyses on their own.

Generally, the supervisor generates five to six overall questions growing out of the data (e.g., Note the amount of English used during the class period. Are you satisfied with this? What are ways of reducing it?). These questions will be raised in the conference or left with the TA for future discussion.

Conference. After studying the data on their own, the supervisor and TA meet to share their ideas. Classroom activities and interactions are analyzed to provide a basis for continuing or for changing teaching behavior. While students' learning is a subject to be discussed, the teacher's strategies and behavior are given equal importance since change in teaching behavior and growth in the teacher's creativity are central goals in supervision. The conference usually ends with an agreement on one or two instructional strategies or activities that will be worked on by the TA for future improvement.

In addition to the course observation made by the methods instructor and the chairperson, experienced TAs and novice TAs visit one another's classes. In this way, they have several points of view on their teaching and a variety of suggestions to draw on for self-improvement. TAs learn from one another, share ideas, and develop skills in observation through this exchange of classroom visits.

In the 1978 survey TAs were asked to evaluate the usefulness of various types of supervision for improving their teaching.[3] Three of the four most highly rated approaches to supervision and conferences included discussions, whereas written comments on the observed lesson without discussion were less highly valued. A priority of individuals with whom to hold the conference included, in rank order, the methods professor, an experienced teaching assistant, and the chairperson or a novice teaching assistant. It should be pointed out that interactions with *all* these individuals were rated from "very useful" to at least "moderately useful." In informal discussions, TAs have indicated that having different individuals observe their classes reduced the threat and anxiety of just one visit that would report on their teaching. They added that the variety of opinions and viewpoints enriched their ideas on improving their teaching.

It also appears that the TAs prefer a period of time alone to analyze their class session before having a conference. This allows them to formulate their own evaluation and analysis of the class and, thus, to have a more interactive conference with the observer. A self-evaluation instrument has proved useful in giving guidelines for the TAs to consider when evaluating the class on their own.[4]

TAs also prefer a period of solitary reflection on their teaching when they evaluate the supervision done through videotaping of their class. In point of fact, all aspects of the videotaping experience are rated as "very useful" to "useful." In open-ended responses to that section of the questionnaire, teaching assistants indicated that they felt they had learned more from viewing their own class than from hearing about their class from someone else. Moreover, they were able to arrive at objective analysis and judgments by viewing and reviewing the tape as opposed to drawing on their own memory of the class session. Since they were able to develop suggestions for improving their teaching before meeting with the training professor, they felt less defensive about receiving criticisms and suggestions from that individual. Most important, they reported that this type of activity encouraged the development of long-term self-evaluation skills that they have used for continued improvement of teaching on their own.

Future Plans and Prospects

In general, this program for training and supervising teaching assistants has been very effective and successful. Nevertheless, several aspects of the program are under consideration for improvement and change in the future. The orientation session is likely to be increased to four or even five days. Those additional days will be devoted to more microteaching by students. That is, TAs will try to teach different kinds of lessons to one another. TAs have reported that this would be realistic and helpful preparation for the first few weeks of classes. Specifically, we envision microteaching as a dialogue, a pattern practice, and a reading lesson. Before teaching a lesson, TAs would view tapes of each type of lesson and would analyze them, using performance criteria as guides.[5] Then all TAs would prepare a ten-minute lesson of a given type (e.g., a pattern practice) to teach to the group. It is hoped that we can videotape these lessons for continued analysis. At the least, the methods instructor and other TAs would give follow-up suggestions for improving the presentation.

In light of the positive response to videotaping classes, we plan to have TAs tape their classes several times during a semester. The first two times, the tape would be viewed only by the TA for purposes of self-evaluation and improvement. Succeeding tapes would be viewed first by the TA and then by the methods instructor or course chairperson with a follow-up conference planned for the two to exchange critiques of the lesson. Additional opportunities for taping would be available to TAs who expressed interest in them.

We are also considering a follow-up methods course to College Teaching of French. TAs have pointed out that the weekly discussions and assignments in the course during their first semester are extremely beneficial for giving them structured and systematic training for teaching. Continued help is needed for teaching the second-semester French course. Training could also be included for the teaching of literature and of conversation courses. These are assignments that newly appointed instructors or assistant professors often receive, yet they have little, if any, training in how to teach such courses.

Finally, serious consideration is being given to hiring a coordinator for the first four semesters of French. Presently, faculty members are assigned to chair one of these courses for a year or two. Then another professor takes on that assignment. Continuity in planning is difficult to achieve when such continual change takes place. Articulation is also difficult to work out when four different people are chairing the courses. Moreover, most of the faculty have their training and major interest in the field of literary research and analysis, not in language teaching. While they have taken on these duties with good intentions and cooperation, they admit that course coordination and supervision take an inordinate amount of energy and reduce the time that they can spend on their research. Finding a specialist in language teaching whose interests lie in researching second-language acquisition and pedagogy would allow us to draw on the expertise of that person and would, at the same time, permit that individual to pursue research in his or her area of interest. Such a person would be able to reinforce the ideas and insights from the methods course and would extend the training of TAs throughout their graduate years at the university.

Summary

This paper has attempted to describe the organization, content, and experiences planned for training and supervising TAs so that they can carry out their roles and responsibilities with assurance and some expertise. Obviously, each department would have to pick and choose among the suggestions to find those which would be most beneficial to its own graduate students, but one cannot stress enough the importance and value of training graduate students to plan lessons that meet the learning needs of their students and to examine and analyze the lessons to see if those needs are being met. A systematic program of TA training and supervision must be established if one hopes to ensure continually improved teaching by the TAs and increased learning by their students.

Notes

[1] For an extended discussion of the findings from this survey, see Anne G. Nerenz, Carol A. Herron, and Constance K. Knop, "The Training of Graduate Teaching Assistants in Foreign Languages: A Review of the Literature and a Description of Contemporary Programs," *French Review*, 52 (1979), 873–88.

[2] For more information on clinical supervision, see Robert Goldhammer, *Clinical Supervision* (New York: Holt, 1969), and Maurice Cogan, *Clinical Supervision* (Boston: Houghton Mifflin, 1973).

[3] See Nerenz et al., p. 886.

[4] See Constance K. Knop, "Developing a Model for Student Teacher Supervision," *Foreign Language Annals*, 10 (1977), 635.

[5] See Constance K. Knop, "The Supervision of Foreign Language Teachers," in *Learning a Second Language*, ed. Frank M. Grittner, Yearbook of the National Society for the Study of Education, 79 (Chicago: Univ. of Chicago Press, 1980), p. 196.